Sundancers
and
River Demons

Sundancers and River Demons

ESSAYS ON LANDSCAPE AND RITUAL

CONGER BEASLEY, JR.

THE UNIVERSITY OF ARKANSAS PRESS

FAYETTEVILLE   LONDON   1990

Designer: Chiquita Babb
Typeface: Linotron 202 Weiss
Typesetter: G & S Typesetters, Inc.
Printer: Braun-Brumfield, Inc.
Binder: Braun-Brumfield, Inc.

The paper used in this publication meets the minimum require-
ments of the American National Standard for Permanence of Paper
for Printed Library Materials
Z39.48-1984. ∞

Earlier versions of these essays appeared in the following publica-
tions: "Blood for the Sun" first published in the "Outlook" section
of the Washington *Post* July 16, 1984, reprinted in *From the Heart-
lands: Photos and Essays from the Midwest*, Bottom Dog Press, Huron,
Ohio, 1988; "The Mongrel Islands" *The North American Review*, De-
cember 1987; "A Black Hills Encounter" *The North American Review*,
March 1985; "The Return of Beaver to the Missouri River" first
published in *Antaeus 57*, Winter 1987, reprinted in *On Nature: Nature, Landscape and Natural History*, North Point Press, San Francisco,
1987; "A Float Trip on the Suwannee River," *Orion Nature Quarterly*,
Winter 1988.

Library of Congress Cataloging-in-Publication Data
Beasley, Conger.
    Sundancers and river demons : essays on landscape and ritual /
Conger Beasley, Jr.
        p. cm.
    ISBN 1-55728-129-7. — ISBN 1-55728-130-0 (pbk.)
    1. West (U.S.)—Description and travel—1981–   2. Ca-
ribbean Area—Description and travel—1981–   3. Natural
History—West (U.S.)   4. Natural history—Caribbean Area.
5. Landscape—West (U.S.) 6. Landscape—Caribbean Area.
7. Beasley, Conger—Journeys—West (U.S.)   8. Beasley,
Conger—Journeys—Caribbean Area.
F595.3.B43   1990
917.8—dc20   89-5168
                                                        CIP

for Betsy

*The earth's dark greatness still expresses
itself in undeciphered languages.*

John Hay

Contents

Preface

One time I found myself out in the middle of the Painted Desert on a lovely summer day. I had dropped off the rim of an overlook at Petrified Forest National Park and was heading north on foot over the peeled and blistered terrain toward the boundary of the Navajo Indian Reservation. I was alone. After a while a curious sensation crept over me. I felt as if the blazing sun and delicate air were conspiring to pull the skull away from my brain. The sensation was unnerving. I felt vulnerable and exposed. I remember thinking how convenient it would be to possess heavy claws like a badger so I could burrow into the solid red earth to escape the spectacle of the empty desert.

Landscape is a powerful catalyst upon the imagination. There are few pleasures more challenging than stepping off into an unfamiliar place and letting the force of the elements work its fingers through the fabric of your identity, prodding and dissolving, jostling and rearranging. The effect is salutary: landscape as a kind of cutting board upon which the identity is dissected and then fused back together into a new amalgam.

The essays in this book evoke a specific sense of

place. They are narratives of encounters set against an expanding backdrop of memory and imagination. Despite how intensely we may feel about the features of a landscape, they do not belong to us. We note their particulars and register their locations in the circle of living things of which they form a part. We also note the emotional impact they make upon our hearts and senses. It is an exchange, not only of information, but of energy and affection. It is available to anyone with the curiosity to delve and explore. It is one of the splendid gifts of being alive.

Sundancers
and
River Demons

The Mongrel Islands

My first morning on Grand Turk Island a donkey wandered into the yard of the Salt Raker Inn and began to chew the rubbery leaves of a tropical plant. I was shaving at the time and glanced out the shuttered window to assess the weather. The donkey was scruffy, with a nappy, caramel-colored hide and floppy ears that drooped over a bony face like a pair of mismatched socks. With great deliberation it crunched several leaves between its yellow teeth and gazed at me with a quizzical expression. Then it stepped toward the window, perhaps to determine if I had anything to offer. "Sorry, pal," I murmured. The donkey snorted and went back to the tree.

Grand Turk is a different place, as far removed from the stereotypical Caribbean paradise as can be imagined. Clustered at the foot of the Bahamian archipelago, eighty miles north of the island of Hispaniola (containing Haiti and the Dominican Republic), are more than forty low, flat, scrubby, coral protrusions, officially belonging to the British government and collectively known as the Turks and Caicos Islands. Grand Turk is the capital and administrative center of this scattered complex. Six miles long by two miles wide, Grand Turk boasts a population of four thousand people, most of whom rely upon Her Majesty's government for economic support.

My first view of the island wasn't especially appealing. A narrow trough of deep water separates Grand Turk from the Caicos Islands to the west. As the aircraft banked over the cobalt-blue depths, I caught a glimpse of a squat, pork chop−shaped wedge of land, apparently devoid of trees and prominent features. A narrow ridge runs from north to south like a buffer wall a few yards from the Atlantic coast. Matted along its slopes with a thick growth of shrubs, the ridge forms the highest point on the island.

The lowlands of the interior are occupied by a glittery salina, or salt pool. Well into the twentieth century this salina and a similar one on nearby Salt Cay provided the primary economic resource for the islands. Channels cut to the ocean permitted salt water at high tide to inundate portions of the interior, choking off all growth and life. Fanned by tall, creaky windmills, the water quickly evaporated in the hot sun. The residue of crunchy salt particles was then raked into piles and sold to Canadian and Bermudan fishermen as a preservative for their stocks of cod, halibut, and haddock.

With the invention of refrigerated cargo holds, the modest industry collapsed, and today the salinas are no longer farmed; they ooze across the desolate landscape like opaque cataracts, garish, ugly tracts of dead

4

water where nothing grows and no one cares to go.
From the ridge on the Atlantic side, looking west into
the afternoon sun, the Grand Turk salina resembles a
pool of glittery phlegm. A fetid odor drifts over the
town. Nothing lives for very long in this slime.

A local historian claims that the island was once rich
with subtropical vegetation. Where the salina stands
today was an inland lagoon, fringed with palm trees
and marshes, commodious enough to shelter ocean-
going ships. In the early 1800s Bermudan entrepreneurs
descended upon the island, cut down the trees, and
destroyed the delicate balance between freshwater
sources and those from the sea. The result was an ecological disaster that turned Grand Turk into an arid
blight of shadeless stone and stagnant water. In return,
the Bermudans built several sturdy old homes out of
Canadian timber like the one that now serves as the
main building of the Salt Raker Inn.

My first night at the Salt Raker I met an Englishman
named Douglas Houseman. I confess a weakness for
anachronisms, and this fellow was clearly one; he appeared to have stepped out of the pages of the Somerset Maugham novel I was reading. He sported a bristly
mustache with the tips honed to rapier points; his eyes
were moist and cerulean blue; he spoke with an impec-
cable Oxbridge accent. He was a bit down on his luck
and had been for some time; we talked about money
for a while, and how it had always seemed to elude
him.

He had a distinguished war record, details of which
were still hush-hush, something about aiding Greek
partisans on Crete in their struggle against the Ger-
mans. For the price of a few beers, he regaled me with
stories, not only about his wartime exploits but about
Middle Caicos, a largely uninhabited island west of
Grand Turk where he had lived for several years.

"It's a perfectly splendid place, you know, pristine

and unspoiled," he enthused, his blue eyes sparking. "The people speak a patois, of which not even they know the origins, and which takes some getting used to. There are coves and anchorages too numerous to count, tall limestone cliffs concealing secret caves, miles of beaches on which no human foot has ever set, and vegetation of a variety and density that makes Grand Turk resemble the Gobi Desert. And the beauty of it is that the place is hard to get to, and once you're there there's virtually no place to stay. So, no tourists with any of their rigamarole and claptrap. If you go to Middle Caicos, you're serious about seeing the place."

I learned a lot from Douglas that first night. Development on the Turks and Caicos Islands, even by Caribbean standards, has been painfully slow. In the last decade Providenciales Island in the Caicos group, located a hundred miles west of Grand Turk, has enjoyed something of a boom. A Club Med has opened, along with several other resorts. Anyone seeking the conventional amenities of the ordinary tropical spa goes there. They do not go to Grand Turk, which has only a few rustic inns like the Salt Raker, scattered along the west coast within easy walking distance of the modest quai and the government offices downtown.

One reason I like islands is that, unlike continents, their landmass is easily traversible. Grand Turk lends itself to exploration by bicycle rather than on foot, though once it has been crossed there's little to return to for a second look. The southern tip features the remains of an old fort, a shady copse of Australian pines, and a sheltered cove that has protected ships since Columbus's time and probably long before that. The north end has an abandoned lighthouse and several buildings that once comprised a U.S. naval installation. In the 1960s NASA erected a tracking station, which, in conjunction with the naval base, helped bolster the fragile economy. When both pulled out in the 1970s, a depression struck from which the island has not yet recovered.

The star attraction for future tourism might be the beautiful seas that lap the coasts. A few hundred yards off the west coast of Grand Turk the pellucid Caribbean plunges from a depth of forty feet to well over a mile. The change in color is dramatic; the creamy sand vanishes abruptly into an inky trough that would chill the imagination of Herman Melville. Along the edge of this spectacular drop-off, shy creatures rising from the depths are frequently observed by scuba divers.

It was fun to sit in the Salt Raker bar and have a drink and listen to the local gossip. Islands like Grand Turk are a lot like small Midwestern towns; if you wait long enough, you can find out a lot about them. Even the normally reticent British were eager to converse with a new face. Over dinner one night a Foreign Service veteran of thirty years reminisced fondly about his early tours in Equatorial Africa in the days before independence when British officials dressed in black tie for dinner. He despised the Turks and Caicos Islands for the inefficiency of its government and the relentless stupidity of the natives. "No one knows how to administer colonies anymore," he sighed ruefully. "And there's really no place left where they can go and learn."

It was from this man that I heard about Salt Cay, which I flew over to the following day. It was a five minute flight over a shallow channel threaded with slimy strips of red algae and splotched with pan shoals and coral heads. I was the only passenger aboard the twin-engine craft. The deep trough of Grand Turk Channel glowed in the bright sun like a slab of marble. Salt Cay, shaped like an isosceles triangle pointing east toward the Atlantic, looked bleak and hot and treeless. It was smaller than Grand Turk, maybe half the size. The main settlement of four hundred people was strung along the thin, sandy margin of the west coast.

I like distant, out-of-the-way places, and it looked as if I had found one. From the air the place looked like the least appealing island I had ever seen in the Caribbean. The pilot buzzed the airstrip—a narrow track gouged out of oolitic limestone—to shoo away the donkeys foraging at the edges. A few minutes later the plane landed with a bounce, the wheels groaning in protest.

I ate a big breakfast at Lovelace's, a rustic little hideaway tucked along a splendid stretch of beach that offered a sweeping view across the channel to Grand Turk, seven miles away. The manager of the place, who was also the owner's son, was friendly and helpful; when he saw that I had foolishly forgotten to bring a hat, he loaned me one. I was grateful for the gift when, after a hearty breakfast of pancakes and eggs, I tramped through a humid mass of steamy air into the interior.

The rolling terrain was broken into a series of cascading hills and narrow valleys, thickly matted with spiny shrubs and thorn bushes. Doves and warblers flitted between the branches. Along the rim of a marshy freshwater pond floated a variety of ducks and grebes. Dusty paths, marked by donkey prints, threaded over the hills; by following them I managed to avoid tearing my clothes on the sharp bushes. Paralleling the two-mile-long east coast of Salt Cay was a narrow, humpbacked ridge crowned at one point with the ruins of an old manor house. Panting laboriously, I finally reached the house after a hard climb and was rewarded with a crow's-nest view of the entire island.

Sunlight seemed to spill from directly overhead with liquid force, smearing the sky, all the way to the horizon, with a bright yellow glare. The view was stunning: stark white beaches fringed the coastline; the dark shroud of South Caicos Island loomed on the western rim of the sea; between the ridge and the coastal settlement, glowing like the milky scales of a dead fish, was an abandoned salina. Up on the ridge, scattered throughout the empty rooms of the ruined house, was an amazing amount of glass and pottery and china shards; long ago, someone had entertained quite lavishly on this isolated rock eyrie.

I had neglected to bring a canteen, and after an hour my mouth was parched. A refreshing wind blew in from the Atlantic, which unfortunately dwindled as I clumped down the leeward side of the ridge in the direction of the salina and the settlement. The west side of the ridge was bounded with rock walls, marking property lines; I followed one down to the lowlands, where I was immediately engulfed in a wash of damp heat. Two donkeys watched me curiously from a patch of shrubs. They seemed the true inhabitants of the island, the rightful inheritors of whatever legacy this barren place had to offer. The expressions on their faces were faintly puzzled. After thrashing for another hour through tangled brush, finding paths and then losing them, startling flocks of small doves into flight with a fluttery rush of wings, I began to wonder too. Finally, I intersected an automobile track leading into town and trudged along it, past gaily painted houses with tin roofs and gnarly hibiscus trees flowering in stony yards.

By this time it was early afternoon and the sun flamed overhead like a merciless beacon, illuminating every bush and rock. I felt squishy and swollen and damp all over. Compared to Grand Turk, the streets of

9

Salt Cay were tidy and well-kept. At this time of day there was nothing astir; I felt like a cowpoke invading a ghost town. A cat snoozed fitfully in a sliver of shade cast by a tilted tombstone in a neglected graveyard by the sea. A light wind turned the rotting blades of an old windmill in the center of the gloomy salina. The main drag paralleling the beach was sparsely fronted by stone and the timber dwellings, with a few cars parked out front, dented and rusty, looking like old turtles that had just climbed out of the sea. Well, this is really the end, I thought. I had found the ultimate backwater province that lurks perpetually at the margins of my imagination and that best evokes the funky Midwestern villages I remember as a boy. It's astounding how these stereotypes, once they take hold, dictate a mode of behavior, a fictive cast of mind, totally out of proportion to their actual meaning and worth. The original images engraved upon the sensitive mind of a child are never really dimmed by experience, but seem to deepen and become more indelible the older one gets. I felt curiously at home on this God-forsaken nub of land. The road leading back to the landscape of my youth seemed to terminate on the bleak, scabby slopes of Salt Cay. I had reached an end of sorts; from here the road dropped off into a bewildering depth of emptiness and desolation, beyond reclamation of either memory or imagination.

The street was deserted; through cloistered doorways, cool and black against the blazing walls, I saw several figures peering out. Mad dogs and Englishmen. The ghost of Mungo Park flits madly at midday through the empty streets of Salt Cay. Who else but a silly white man would subject himself to the rigors of such burning air on an island where few strangers have stepped for the last hundred years? Where the road turned back east toward the airstrip, I encountered a solitary man, dressed as if he were going to church in a clean white shirt, green polyester coat, and checkered trousers, shuffling like a sleepwalker. We stared at one another like survivors of an atomic quake. The heat rose up around us in palpable swells. "What you be doin' out in dis heat t'day, mon?" he asked in a dry, croaky voice.

I had no answer. My mouth was incapable of response. I felt as if a stork had built a nest in my throat. My cheeks were flushed, and a cool tingling, the first sign of heat prostration, danced up and down my arms. I waved listlessly and staggered the rest of the way to Lovelace's where I gulped down three beers and collapsed into a hammock. The manager scolded me for my foolishness. "You don't ever want to walk around by yourself on this island, not even in the moonlight," he declared. I groaned and nodded in agreement. Three hours later, somewhat revitalized, I hobbled to the airstrip and helped a boy throw rocks at the donkeys to clear them off the landing path. Then, weary but satisfied, I boarded an aircraft and roared back through the gathering dusk to Grand Turk.

The following day I remained in a stupor. All morning, as I tried to keep my eyes focused upon the pages of the Somerset Maugham novel, my stomach felt finicky. Right after lunch I got sick. I spent the afternoon sprawled in a lounge chair under the shadow of a porch staring out at the sea. Around two, during the muggiest part of the day, a black man strolled along the narrow rock-walled lane between the Salt Raker Inn and the beach. He wore wrap-around dark glasses, a porkpie hat, white shirt and paisley tie, a beige vest, creamy brown slacks, and blue Adidas tennis shoes. One of those inimitable Caribbean figures, timeless and self-contained, clad in a mishmash of styles, coming from nowhere and going nowhere. In his right

11

hand he carried a sleek metallic briefcase. He walked with a languid strut, pleased, no doubt, to find himself headed downtown on some kind of official business, though in no particular hurry to get there. For a moment, as he passed by the gate, his narrow-brimmed hat bobbed along the line of the horizon like the silhouette of a distant ship.

"It doesn't make any difference what I say to them," John Coulter sighed over dinner at the Salt Raker that night. "They won't do it anyway." He was speaking about the accountants in the department whose books he was auditing. "I don't know whether it's imbecility or perversity, but they can't get it right. Drawing up a simple balance sheet is as taxing to their minds as the mysteries of nuclear fission are to mine. There's simply no instructing them. They are intractable to the point of tears. We all might be better off if a tidal wave wiped out the entire island."

Despite his grumpy disposition, I enjoyed John's company. He was a small man with precise blond features and an appetite for greasy hamburgers, which he consumed every lunch with lip-smacking relish. Afterward, he retired to his room for a nap. Refreshed, he then sallied back downtown to one of the government buildings to oversee the keeping of the books. John lived in Barbados but every three months was forced to make the long flight from Bridgetown to Miami and then back down the Bahamian archipelago to Grand Turk. He had never been anywhere else on the islands, neither Salt Cay nor any of the Caicos. He listened attentively as I told him about my adventure on Salt Cay and smiled grimly as I described the heat and the ubiquitous donkeys.

The following day I had recovered enough to rent a bicycle and pedal to the east side of the island. Beyond the salina, on the outskirts of the native section, stretched an ugly junkyard, heaped and stacked with rusty pipes, appliances, and automobiles. A dirt track branched off the paved road toward the barrier ridge. I followed it and within a quarter mile came to a marsh fringed with green grass, situated in a modest hollow between two limestone knolls. I slipped off the bike and rubbed my eyes. Where had this place come from? Though treeless, it was the most verdant spot on Grand Turk.

Bob Marley music cut through the air with a ragged, lilting beat. I looked around. A man sat on one of the knolls, cradling a boom box and smoking a twisted spliff. Though I was only a few yards away, he paid no attention to me and gazed out toward the calcareous ridge and the Atlantic Ocean. I felt as if I had intruded upon a private sanctuary. Just where does one go to get away from the depressing fact of a limited life on an impoverished island? If Salt Cay had the feeling of being located at the limits of the Caribbean imagination, Grand Turk was the New World promise traduced and undermined by colonial patronage and discrimination. A glum depression stole over me. I had no right, not even for one minute, to share this blissful spot with the man on the knoll. I mounted the bicycle and pedaled back toward the paved road.

Mongrelization is a cultural reality of most Caribbean islands, composed, as they are, of contrasting European and African elements. (The Native American presence, ruthlessly purged by Columbus and his followers, is barely detectable.) Unlike Haiti or Jamaica, whose disparate backgrounds have merged to create New World amalgams, the people of the Turks and Caicos Islands seem to possess neither rebelliousness nor a well-developed sense of acquiescence that might make them over into clones of their masters. Desultory occupation by the Spanish, French, and British have given the cultural fabric of the islands a patchwork complexion, with no single influence predominating. For a while in the nineteenth century the islands were administered by Bermuda; for several decades in this century Jamaica assumed control. Evidently this is a place that nobody wants, that has no exploitable resources, that offers little promise for a future, that seems destined to remain a squalid backwater outpost.

Currently a ponderous bureaucratic apparatus lies like a heavy lid over the top of this provincial dustbin, though even if it were removed there is little guarantee that anything indigenous or nationalistic might rise to the surface. Grand Turk and Salt Cay are not so much representative of the Third World as they are of a dreary classification of colonial trusts seemingly incapable, for economic reasons, of steering their own course amid the perils of the contemporary world. If the French ran the island, there would be a decent restaurant or two; the Spanish would make sure that certain festival days were celebrated; but under the dour hand of the British the islanders are treated like poor relatives, uneducable above their present status, an embarrassment, not only to their fellow colonials on Anguilla, Montserrat, and Grand Cayman, but to their bolder, independent, and more successful black compatriots in the Caribbean.

From all evidence the people appear resigned to a drab fate, stoically inured to living out their lives in a poverty of expectations, like clams baking under a ruthless sun. No doubt there are subterranean political forces brewing under the dull glaze of resignation, but with nothing to fuel them, nothing to give them voice, no energy or consciousness or motivating intelli-

14

gence to give them form or recognition, the likelihood of their ever emerging seems dim indeed. "There's no such thing as a 'usable past' here," Douglas Houseman lamented, "These people don't even have a history. How then are they to know what it is they need to react against? It's the classic New World dilemma, exaggerated to an absurd degree, with everything that might be of potential meaning diminished to the point of invisibility, as if viewed through the wrong end of a telescope."

One evening an energetic group gathered at the Salt Raker for drinks and dinner, a mixed bag of engineers, foreign officers, and local characters. Other than myself and a woman from Guyana, there were no tourists. The engineers were constructing a desalinization plant on the island to help ease the water supply problem. "Holiday Inn wants to build a big complex here," one engineer said, "but until the water problem is solved they won't invest a penny. Years ago the only water the islanders had was from cisterns and catch basins and what they could draw out of wells. Today they have the wells and the desalinization plant, but that's not nearly enough to meet the demands that a Holiday Inn would create."

While John Coulter, the Guyanese woman, and I ate dinner, Douglas Houseman remained alone at the bar, nursing a beer and sifting through a stack of mail. The Salt Raker Inn was his official P.O. box on Grand Turk, and for a man who appeared to have few friends and virtually no family, he certainly received a lot of mail. "Poor Doug," John sighed through a mouthful of spicy chicken. "The stories about his partisan exploits are absolutely true, you know. He had some incredible adventures. He was a full colonel at age twenty-three, and after the war was honored by the Greek government. That's a tough act to follow. Must make the rest of one's life seem rather anticlimactic."

After dinner more people arrived. The bar did a brisk business; instead of turning out the lights by eight P.M., as was usual on a Wednesday evening, Graham Barker, the manager, was busy mixing drinks, pouring wine, and opening beers. By nine the dinner hubbub had intensified to a cocktail party buzz. John Coulter introduced me to a prominent official in the government, a short, robust, thickset man with curly hair and a square, sanguine face named David Long. David had the disconcerting habit of squeezing his eyes shut whenever he addressed me, whether out of shyness or arrogance or a sharp spell of gas I couldn't tell.

He was adamant, despite evidence to the contrary (including a recent *National Geographic* article), that Grand Turk, and not San Salvador Island or Samana Cay in the Bahamas, was the site of Columbus's first landfall in the New World. He cited evidence from the explorer's journals and declared that at a future date a team of Spanish historians would reveal the results of an exhaustive survey on the subject. "We are definitely a contender for the five hundredth anniversary sweepstakes in 1992," he concluded, lowering his eyelids and rolling his head oddly about. "Grand Turk has a lot going for it in that department. In fact, where we are sitting right now could well be the exact spot where Columbus first set foot on American soil."

The hairs on the back of my neck bristled in response.

"This is no bit of idle speculation!" David barked. "We know that he first spotted the island from the Atlantic side, but that he then sailed around to the west coast in order to escape the heavy surf. The other islands that he mentions as being visible from Grand Turk tally perfectly today. From the mast of a good-sized

16

vessel at the south cove, for instance, an observer can see Salt Cay, Cotton Cay, South and Middle Caicos. Yes, I think we have a very strong case, which our ministry of tourism intends to capitalize upon. You Americans can blather all you like about San Salvador or Samana Cay or any other island in the Bahamas. We're convinced that it was right here."

The evening bumped on. People came and went. An attractive mulatto with a guitar entered with an entourage of white civil servants, sang one song, and disappeared. Around ten, slightly tipsy, I found myself on the beach in front of the Salt Raker with the Guyanese woman. She was from England, and had married a doctor from Georgetown and lived there for thirty years. She was tall and handsome with well-formed hands. Her nursing specialty was leprosy. In a dry, reticent voice she described the symptoms of the disease, the way the victims' fingers wither and vanish, how their faces curl up in dessicated strips like paint on a wall.

"You've been away from England for a long time," I said. "Do you miss it? Would you like someday to retire there?"

"I dream of England nearly every night now," she replied. "Especially of the rolling countryside of West Suffolk where I was raised. All my family there is gone, except one distant cousin with whom I still correspond. My husband died last year, and my son now lives in Miami. I suspect, when the time comes for me to retire, that I will join him there."

A tall figure emerged from the front gate of the Salt Raker and ambled across the narrow lane to the beach. "Good evening, Douglas," I called.

"Ah well, it's you, is it?"

The voice cut through the moist air with the vibrato of a tuning fork. Moonlight shimmered against the beach; lemon-colored waves broke with a gentle slush against the sand. I could discern the whites of Douglas's eyes and the flamboyant silhouette of his mustache. "Well, it's pleasant enough to be out, eh?" he called.

"Indeed it is."

There was a pause; then he added, "I never tire of it, you know. Moonlight like this. White combers charging to shore like stallions. And the air. My God, it's practically drinkable!"

A few clouds floated overhead, but for the most part the sky was clear. To the west, trailing down to the horizon like a cluster of grapes, was a mass of palpitating stars. A three-quarters moon drifted over the barrier ridge, sheening the arid ground, the dusky town, in a metallic light. In the yard next to the Salt Raker, a donkey stretched its scruffy neck over a rock wall to nibble the blossoms off a bougainvillea.

"Well, then," Douglas called. "Cheerio. It's time I was off to bed."

"Pleasant dreams," I called.

"I've never dreamed a single night since I've lived on these islands," he confessed. "When you live in paradise, there's really nothing much to dream about, is there?"

I got sick again for a couple of days, biliously sick. The alkaline content of the water on Grand Turk affects even the most experienced travelers; veterans like John Coulter come equipped with an arsenal of medicine. Other than a bottle of aspirin, I was totally unprepared. There was nothing in the downtown stores except a few bottles of Pepto-Bismol and packets of Rolaids. Graham Barker loaned me some powerful pills, manufactured in England, from his private stock. By the end of the second day I was on the mend.

For those two days I lay in a torpid half-daze on a lounge chair in the porch shade with a pleasant view of the sea, and indoors during the afternoon, glazed with

18

perspiration, in a pool of gummy air riffled by the ceiling fan. I read and slept and slept and read. People and cars passed one way down the lane toward town in the morning. In the afternoon they returned, the pedestrians, that is; all vehicles were routed out of town on a street alongside the salina. With an afternoon breeze stirring the casurina trees, their voices, high-pitched and melodious, sounded like tropical birds dimly heard through a screen of leaves.

One morning near the end of my stay I awoke to find the western sky ascowl with clouds and a stiff wind whipping the sea into a lathery foam. Out on the beach I watched a lateen-rigged Haitian boat pitch away from the storm toward the protected cove at the south tip of the island. Two donkeys trotted out of the rainy air, crossed the lane, and began cropping the vines and sea oats tufting the beach. One clomped up and nudged my arm. "What's up, pal?" I muttered. The beast stared at me blankly, not expecting anything yet ready for any gift that might come its way. When I reached out to stroke its nose, it snorted rudely and clattered away.

A small boat moored to a buoy had overturned in the high seas, and several young British civil servants stood on the beach discussing the best way to salvage it. I joined them, and after some debate we decided to strip down and swim out to see what we could do. The buoy was a good hundred yards from shore, and a half-dozen of us paddled through unseasonably cool water into the teeth of a ripping wind. Despite the swells that pitched us about like corks, we managed to righten the boat and attach a cable to the bow. The cable stretched to a truck parked on the beach; with a grating whine the winch on the rear bumper began to turn and within minutes the boat was high and dry on the sand.

It was Sunday morning and the locals were walking

or bicycling along the narrow lane to the Anglican Church in town. They were dressed in their best finery, the men in dark suits, the women in white-starched skirts, all of them carrying Bibles. The swimmers had just returned to the beach and were drying off when a long black automobile with twin Union Jack pennants rippling from the fenders slowed to a halt, and from the back seat, resplendently clad in a crisp white uniform and pith helmet, stepped the governor-general of the island. "I say, everything all right here?" he called.

"Oh, yes sir, yes sir," several voices chorused at once. "Everything's under control."

"Jolly good then. Carry on."

The car disappeared down the lane. I finished toweling off and slipped on a pair of trousers. Out to sea the Haitian boat continued to bob south, its tattered sail gleaming like a silver wing against the glowering clouds. The Brits invited me to the Salt Raker for a beer, but I declined. They were a boisterous, spirited bunch; several were on holiday and had come out to Grand Turk to cheer up friends stationed at this lonely remnant of a vanished empire. They spoke of the fun they had had in grandiloquent terms, as only people can who are accustomed, by temperament and habit, to using impoverished places as catalysts for private fantasies.

Silently, with little fanfare, as mysteriously as phantoms, the locals, singly and in modest groups, continued to plod down the lane toward town, oblivious of the British and their friends, like extras in a play with no costumes, little drama, and nothing at all to say.

A Float Trip
on the Suwannee River

Maybe it was a good omen after all.

Durward and I had stopped at the Stephen Foster
Folk Center in White Springs to view the Suwannee
River, and I was leading the way down a steep flight of
steps when something coiled around my right shoe
and spun off into the weeds. At first I thought my laces
had come untied, but then I realized it was a green
snake, common to north Florida, whose path had
crossed unexpectedly with mine. The pressure of its
lithe body around my foot—a touch so subtle as to be
almost evanescent—sent a chill up my spine. Encounters with snakes are always momentous. They shrink
one's feelings to a pinpoint of vestigial fear. "Who's
your friend?" Durward said jokingly. I shrugged and
danced nervously down the rest of the steps.

There I was. On the bank of a placid, subtropical river that had teased my imagination since I was a boy. The dense, opaque color made me chuckle. No other river that I knew of looked quite like this. On this warm, windless afternoon it glimmered like a chunk of polished onyx. The foliage overhead was minutely reflected in the smooth surface. It looked hard enough to rollerskate across. I knelt down and dipped my fingers into the current. The water was soft and pleasing to touch. My fingers were coated with a cinnamon tinge. A few inches deeper and they disappeared.

Upriver from White Springs, all the way to its source in Georgia, the Suwannee is unpolluted by industrial synthetics. Its current is fed, not by ancillary streams, but by hidden springs. There is something appealing about a river that looks one way and feels another. But that is part of the Suwannee's charm. Tannic acid leaching through the soil from decomposing pine needles and live oak leaves gives the water its unique coloration. That is the scientific explanation. Left alone long enough upon its brooding surface, the imagination can conjour up a variety of explanations, some plausible, some fantastical.

Long ago, so the story goes, the Seminole Indians were ruled by a woman chief, Su-wan-nee, whose name was eventually given to the river so that her spirit might live on in dignity and honor. One good story invariably gives rise to another. Early Spanish explorers called the river the Little St. Johns to distinguish it from the Big St. Johns lying to the east. When English-speaking settlers arrived in Florida in the eighteenth century, they corrupted the name San Juanito to the more colloquial "Suwannee."

The Suwannee rises in the depths of the Okefenokee Swamp of southeast Georgia. It crawls sluggishly across the Florida line then bends and hooks and

22

doubles-back in a diagonal path across the northern third of the state to the Gulf of Mexico. Along the more than two hundred miles of its course, it passes no settlement of any major size, only modest villages and towns. That, somehow, is in keeping with its character. The Suwannee is a private, secretive river. While almost everyone has heard of it, thanks to Stephen Foster's song, few people know what it looks like or can describe it with any accuracy.

"Of all the rivers in America the Suwannee is the most romantic," declares writer Cecile Hulse Matschat. After floating down it in a canoe for five days, sleeping under a full moon, I would have to agree. Some rivers inspire the imagination, others personify it. With all its moods and colors, the Suwannee seems to have emerged directly from the emotional depths of the Romantic sensibility. The English poet Samuel Taylor Coleridge apparently thought so, and like Stephen Foster he never laid eyes on the river. An early account of north Florida published in the 1790s by William Bartram so intrigued Coleridge that he transcribed entire passages in his notebook. The effect of Bartram's descriptions of the lush flora upon his imagination was alchemical. The images nourished his own potent dream life and helped inspire the exotic metaphors of poems like "Kubla Khan" and "The Rime of the Ancient Mariner."

My companion for the five-day excursion was a lanky, retired Air Force officer named Durward Young. Durward lived in Albuquerque and had floated many rivers of the Southwest. He was experienced and capable; he could cook and fix things; he was cautious and efficient. He liked to tell stories and sit by a campfire and watch the flames swirl up into the air. He played the harmonica and could wheeze out a repertory of familiar tunes to help pass the lonely hours.

Comfortably settled into two sixteen-foot canoes
laden with food and camping equipment, we put on
the river at a spot approximately fifteen miles north of
the town of Fargo, Georgia, on the edge of the Okefenokee. The time was mid-April; four days of torren-
tial rain the previous week had expanded the width of
the already sizeable channel. The morning of the first
day Durward and I picked our way through a labyrinth
of rivulets and backwaters, crashing through brambles
and thickets, fearful of knocking a cottonmouth snake
down into our canoes. Gaudy butterflies and iridescent
dragonflies danced about our heads and alighted on
our knees. We paid keen attention to the slightest
trace of a current and were careful not to become too
distantly separated as we forged through the drowned
terrain.

Our first campsite was a dandy. Amid the morass of
spreading water and hammocks of impenetrable vegetation, we came upon a hunk of solid ground sloping
out of the stream to a stand of slash pines. It was early
afternoon, but the sight was too appealing to pass
up. We pitched our tents on a crunchy bed of pine
needles, built a fire, drank hot tea and cocoa, swapped
jokes and stories. At sundown a grizzled man in a battered pickup rattled down a path between the trees.
He was the proprietor of the land. He was cordial but
guarded, the way a monk might be if you entered his
monastery bearing firecrackers and a bullhorn. We assured him that our intentions were honorable, and we
offered to leave straightaway if our presence was offen-
sive. No, he liked to think of himself as a Christian
man. (The woman sitting beside him in the pickup
nodded vigorously at this assertion.) Provided we
picked up our trash and didn't burn the trees down, he
had no quarrel with our staying. An expression lurked
in the depths of the man's eyes that bespoke a certain

24

tenacity and stubbornness. "My people have lived in this swamp for longer than I can count," he revealed. "We're an easy people, slow to rile. The only rift we ever suffered was one time before I was born when a party of us witnessed right here at this landing huge chunks of ice come floating down the stream. It was a Sunday afternoon. My daddy was present, and this story was handed on to me by him. All the folks that was here, including my daddy, thought the ice was a revelation from God. Where else could ice have come from in this swamp in mid-July? It had to be a sign from the Almighty. Of what though, nobody seemed to know. Well, when they took the story to church that evening, the quarrels started in. Those that hadn't seen the miracle, and that had lived all their lives here, couldn't believe it. The church split right down the middle in two factions, the Ice Baptists and the No-Ice Baptists. I guess things stayed pretty heated for a long while. Got so bad even, the Ice Baptists took to setting on one side of the aisle, the No-Ice on the other . . ."

Many times during the next two days I gazed up enviously at the turkey vultures and white ibises and rancorous crows floating high over the trees. If only they could tell us where we were, I thought. We had a map, though many of the landmarks pinpointed on it had a way of not showing up when they were supposed to. From their lofty elevation, the birds could easily detect our position. Down below, hemmed in by dark foliage and towering trees, Durward and I floundered about like moles in a maze of leafy tunnels.

The second night we slept on a soggy spit between the river and a spongy pine copse. As the sun paled between the trees, clouds of mosquitoes assailed us. Shortly after supper we were driven inside our tents. I puffed a Jamaican cigar, stunning the varmints that buzzed under the netting and half-asphyxiating myself.

25

Around eight a bright moon eased over the ragged silhouette of trees lining the east bank. As if on cue, the beams of light spangling the river's indigo surface triggered a dazzling outburst of sounds. A barred owl hooted thunderously from a nearby tree. Insects made ferocious grinding noises. Leopard frogs croaked with stereophonic fervor. A chuck-will's-widow whistled piercingly.

Inside my tent I lay perfectly still, hoping I wouldn't be noticed. How different in volume and intensity these noises were compared to the western rivers—the Green, the San Juan, the Colorado—that Durward and I had floated together. The birds sounded as if they were sitting on top of my tent. The leopard frog seemed to be concealed inside my boot. Despite the mosquitoes, I unzipped the flap and peered out. The brightness of the moon had reduced the river and the trees on the opposite bank to solid black forms. There was something massive and forbidding about them. They were like chunks of stygian darkness, congealed into dense blocks and winched up from the bowels of the underworld to decorate the set of some gloomy Elizabethan play.

This was an illusion, of course. Once the moon waned and the eastern horizon started to pale, the scene would be transformed. But that, too, was part of the Suwannee's appeal; the interplay between darkness and light was always changing, always evolving into something unexpected and surprising. The lure was irresistible; it worked upon the senses with a physical effect, hinting at the possibility of a deeper emotional attachment—the discovery of new links, new correspondences—between the imagination and this evocative terrain.

Had Coleridge been with us that night, I wonder how he would have described the sounds and swaddled darkness and moon-spangled river gurgling a few feet from our tents? Despite the howling birds and spooky atmosphere, I managed to fall asleep. In addition to being romantic, the Suwannee is also paradoxical—scary on the one hand, soothing on the other. At the same time my imagination conjured all sorts of terrifying creatures outside my tent flap, my body sank into an uneasy slumber. Amid the bird whistles and animal hoots, I could hear Durward blissfully snoring. It was evident that at the heart of this subtropic wilderness there existed a kind of refuge that enfolded us peaceably in its arms.

According to William Bartram, a secret kingdom of beautiful women and fierce hunters once lurked at the heart of the Okefenokee Swamp. Hunters from a neighboring Creek tribe, lost in the swamp, were often rescued by these beautiful women. They were taken in, fed and succored, and all-too-soon forced to leave before the jealous husbands returned from their hunt. The place where these Indians lived was regarded as the most paradisical spot on earth.

Quite possibly the tale is a sacralized remnant of Creek and Seminole stories of a splinter group of Mayan Indians who long ago journeyed up the Suwannee River, all the way to its source, to establish a kingdom of temples and mounds and earth altars. For centuries the region has been regarded by people as a refuge. The Seminoles—a word that means "runaway"—took to the river and swamps to escape encroaching white settlers. Slaves hid in the wilds to avoid capture by their owners. Confederate deserters, weary of a hopeless war, disappeared into the green depths.

The concept of a refuge has poignant application. Florida, which a century ago was virtually untouched, is today in danger of sinking under the weight of its own development. Even north Florida, the Other Flor-

27

ida, is inexorably being transformed into a familiar exurbia of condominiums and shopping centers. Dwindling wilderness areas like the Suwannee may soon have to be placed under some form of management control in order to preserve what remains of their ecological integrity. Durward and I were enjoying a rare treat, a free-wheeling float upon a marvelous river unhindered by the rules and regulations that govern human traffic on, say, the majority of rivers in the Southwest.

The next day, our third, we finally spotted a definite landmark—the little town of Fargo, Georgia. A woman reading a book in a bankside park barely looked up as we drifted by. I gazed wistfully at her curvaceous figure, and then turned my attention to more important matters downstream. She was the only human being we saw until we reached our destination of White Springs. We passed under a couple of bridges empty of traffic. Only one telephone line spanned the river during the entire sixty-five—mile length of our journey.

Our primary companions were crows and turkey vultures. Kingfishers chattered scoldingly as they flew between the banks. Mockingbirds gurgled and trilled. Flocks of white ibises dotted the treetops like puffs of cotton. One morning we watched the lean figure of an anhinga lift off the river and soar over our heads on quick wingstrokes. Equally at home in the air or underwater, the anhinga is a graceful creature about which William Bartram observed, "I doubt not but if this bird had been an inhabitant of the Tiber in Ovid's days, it would have furnished him with a subject for some beautiful and entertaining metamorphoses."

South of Fargo, near the Georgia-Florida line, the swamps receded and the river flowed between clearly defined banks. Live oaks, slash pines, and bald cypress lined the water's edge. Bearded coils of Spanish moss drooled from the branches. Clusters of purple wisteria

28

blossomed everywhere, along with pink swatches of wild azalea. Down along the banks, like formidable *chevaux-de-frise*, sprouted stands of yellow-green palmettos.

Bald cypress, their lower trunks swollen with water, soared up through the dark river. Closeby, poking a few feet above the surface, were pointy little knobs, or "knees," which help stabilize the tree and assist it in breathing. Bald cypresses are deciduous conifers that shed their thin, pliable leaves once a year. The soft bark provides an important nesting site for the noisy and colorful pileated woodpecker. An amazingly durable wood, cypress is used for a wide range of building purposes. The wood's renowned resistance to decay has made it useful for everything from gutters to grave markers. Hollow cypress logs installed as water pipes in New Orleans in 1798 were still serviceable when replaced in 1914.

In the winter of 1950, when I was nine years old, my parents pulled my brother and I out of school in Missouri and drove us to Florida for a leisurely stay that lasted five delightful weeks. Crossing north Florida, on the way to the Atlantic coast, we passed over the Suwannee River. As the car rumbled over the bridge I distinctly remember my mother bursting into song. Not the immortal Stephen Foster number, but rather the tune popularized by Al Jolson, who sang it in blackface: "Su-wan-nee . . . How I love ya . . . How I love ya . . . My dear old Su-wan-nee . . ."

Few things are more compelling to a child than the unexpected enthusiasms of his parents. I remember looking at my normally reticent mother in astonishment, and then down at the black river. What exactly was the connection between these two events, cross-

29

ing the bridge and her outburst of song? The rivers in Missouri were muddy and brown. Mother never sang when we crossed them. When I asked out loud why the river was so dark, no one knew the answer. There was a moment of awkward silence. The song on mother's lips trailed off to a whisper. My brother turned grumpily back to his comic book. Other than the ducks and geese he hunted in the fall, my father knew nothing about natural science. It was just that way, his silence seemed to say, just as he was my father and I was his son. Some things like the color of certain rivers were just fated to be, and no amount of explanation could ever make them comprehensible to anyone.

I forgot about the river for a long time, or at least I thought I did. And then, when I was about twelve or thirteen, I began to have a recurring dream. No doubt it was connected to the onslaught of adolescence, though instead of being threatening the dream was soothing and delicious. It featured me adrift in a wide-bellied canoe upon a sleek current that wound through a land similar to north Florida. Subtropical trees cloaked the banks. Spindly-legged birds of colorful plumage flew overhead. A moist breeze, scented with the fragrance of blossoming flowers, blew steadily upstream. So uniform and steady was the current that I rarely had to paddle to maintain my course. In fact I spent most of the time lying down in the canoe with my head pillowed on a cushion. Never in my life, before or since, waking or sleeping, have I ever felt as relaxed as I did in that dream. I hated to wake up in the morning. I hated to open my eyes and relinquish my hold on that lovely sensation.

Once Durward and I had paddled beyond the fringes of the great swamp, the Suwannee was easy to nego-

tiate. Drifting side-by-side in the canoes, we joked
and chatted. Durward played his harmonica while I
looked for birds. The riparian corridor of the Suwannee has long been a refuge for an exotic variety of
birds. For three birds that today are considered ex-
tinct—Bachman's warbler, the Carolina parakeet, and
the ivory-billed woodpecker—it was one of the last
places where they were ever observed. My own personal discovery was a yellow-crowned night heron
that slipped noiselessly over my head one afternoon,
making a beeline downstream.

On every river I've ever floated there is a passage
that lasts a few minutes or several hours and that repre-
sents the heart of the river, that fulfills whatever expectations I might have had of it. Around noon of the
fourth day we rounded a bend, and almost instantly
the texture and color of the Suwannee seemed to take
on a new intensity. A mild wind rippled the strands of
Spanish moss festooning the trees. A warm sun beam-
ing between puffy clouds transformed the river into a
liquid band of black currant jelly. The lucent current
seemed to lose all semblance of water. It became a dis-
tillation of many-shaded foliages, sweeping smoothly
beneath us. It was green trees, fluent.

The recognition was instantaneous. Durward nodded and raised his paddle in salutation. All during the
slow, delicious hour it took to float this section, I
gazed around, astounded. It was as if my childhood
dream about the river had risen magically out of my
subconscious and was flowing unobstructed through
my waking life.

But dreams, like nature, have a way of turning upon
themselves, and even the most indolent moments con-
tain the threat of danger. Periodically during our journey Durward and I had encountered chunks of driftwood. Off the starboard bow of the canoe, fifteen feet
away, I spotted what appeared to be a fair-sized log.

31

Most likely a cypress branch, I thought, and then watched with chilled fascination as the log turned slowly against the current to point straight for me. That's an alligator, a voice whispered in my head. The snout was plainly visible, the notched ridge of the eyes, the broad back, the serrated profile of the tail. At least five feet of the creature was visible, with a lot more concealed underneath. The alligator regarded me for a few moments with a strange, fathomless stare, then sank out of sight.

Like the grizzly bear and the wolf, alligators have been the subject of some pretty strange conjectures. A French officer named Bossu in the 1750s observed a raft of green branches poking up through the water of a southern river and plowing upstream against a swift current with no visible means of locomotion. The black man paddling the pirogue explained that what he was seeing were tiny trees growing out of the back of an alligator. As the pirogue drew close, the alligator plunged into the channel, taking the trees with it. The black man explained that when hunters shot at alligators they frequently made holes in their hard, scaly backs without killing them. The alligators then passed the winter, immobile and torpid, in the oozy mud. In the holes cored by the bullets fell the seeds of willows, tupelo, and cypress with which the river was bordered. The seeds took root in the moss covering the alligators' hides and, favored by moisture, formed the trees the animals carried with them when they emerged in the spring.

That evening Durward and I bathed hastily in the water a few inches from the bank. An hour before reaching camp he had seen his own alligator. The sight had evoked vivid memories of growing up in Louisiana in the 1930s. "A 'gator will grab hold of its victim with an iron clamp of the jaws then roll over and over in the water till the victim drowns," he explained as we sat around the campfire swatting mosquitoes. "In Louisiana there were always stories about people and dogs getting caught. For me, the alligator was the bogeyman. I'm glad they're no longer an endangered species and that they've made such a great comeback, and I'm willing to let them have as much territory as they want. They scare the hell out of me."

That night outside my tent an infernal racket awoke me from a sound sleep. An anguished cry cut through the still air and crashed to the ground in a clatter of steel plates. A light snapped on in Durward's tent. "Good God, man! What was that all about?"

I unzipped the mosquito netting and crawled out of the tent. Durward slumped on a log in front of the embered fire flicking a bandana against his neck and cheeks.

"I found my heart on my chest when I woke up to that one," he confessed. "Something must've gotten killed over there in those trees."

A shiver trembled the length of my spine. The specter of an alligator with green trees growing out its back drifted before my eyes.

"This river's a funny place," Durward muttered. "It's so damn pretty. And yet it's got these thorns hidden in it."

"I used to dream about this river when I was a kid . . ." I went on to tell the story: the long car ride to Florida in 1950, the comfort I experienced floating on the phantom river, the reaction of my own children when I showed them the real river thirty-five years later.

The mosquitoes were fierce, and I continued the story inside my tent, projecting my voice through the netting. There was silence after I finished. I thought Durward had fallen asleep. "Maybe you'd better stay away from this place," he finally said.

"How come?"

33

"It's got its hooks into you. It flows through the center of your life like an aorta. If you followed it all the way to the sea instead of getting off at White Springs, I wonder if you could find your way back."

I thought about the snake that had curled itself around my foot when Durward and I first walked down to inspect the river. So subtly, with such gentle pressure, I hardly even noticed. The Suwannee was that way. Lissome and alluring. Lulling and hypnotic. A river, not of forgetfulness, but of insight and reverie. A river so beautiful at moments in its interplay of current, sunlight, and foliage that the joy of discovery mingled with a pang of inexplicable sorrow.

"Durward!"

"Yo!"

"You still awake?"

"I am now."

"Do alligators crawl ashore after dark?"

"I don't know."

"Help me out, Durward . . ."

"No, they don't. They settle to the bottom of the river and bury themselves in the mud. They're heavy sleepers. You couldn't budge one with a stick of dynamite."

The anxiety that filled my chest began to subside. "Thanks, Durward."

"Don't mention it."

The following afternoon, a few miles from White Springs, we saw our first people since the woman sunning herself on the bank outside Fargo. Two men clad in raingear churned upstream in a johnboat. Fishing poles poked out the bow and stern. We passed one another like ships in a fog, flying unrecognizable flags. The clatter of their outboard engine sounded faintly obscene. They stared at us with dull, uncomprehending faces. We stared back at them. They probably lived around here, and we were strangers. But we had just passed through an experience that was denied to them. They knew the river from habit; they no doubt had fished it before, and besides they were plowing upstream with the aid of a motor, whereas we had drifted with the current. There are few natural forces more compelling than the downward pull of water toward a confluence with the sea.

A few minutes later, we reached the slip cut into the high bank that marked the end of our journey. Durward stepped out and began to unload his equipment. I remained in my canoe, trailing both hands in the water, watching them appear and disappear. Durward heaved his riverbag across his shoulders and climbed the muddy stairs to the top of the bank. "You going to sit there all day?" he called down to me.

"I'd like to. I'd like to do just that."

He looked at me a little sadly. "You can't," he said quietly. "You've got to come with me."

Axel Lindgren
and the Ocean Lady

I was attracted to the man the moment I saw him. He had a fleshy, moon-shaped face, a glittering smile, and nut-colored skin. He wore a maroon windbreaker and a blue New York Mets ballcap. He was bending over a large redwood log chipping away at the interior with a sharp adze-like instrument. The log rested on a triad of pedestals; it was evident that he was shaping some kind of boat. The bow and stern were both squared off; the smooth sides curved down to a stable beam. Wood chips littered the grass.

He stood up from his work and greeted us cordially. His name was Axel Lindgren. He was a boatbuilder. His father had been a boatbuilder, though in the white man's way, with planks and keels and nails. Axel preferred the traditional Yurok method of hollowing out a redwood log. The boat he was presently working on was nearly completed. With its square ends and comfortable beam, it looked sturdy. It had to be, Axel explained, to withstand the rapids on northern California's tumultuous rivers and to plow through the charging sea.

Axel patiently answered all our questions about the boat. Traditionally the redwood canoe was used by the Yurok to harvest shellfish and hunt sea animals. The blunt ends enabled fishermen to paddle up to a rock without banging the hull. At low tide, merely by leaning over the side, they could gather mussels and abalone. The rounded beam made the boat easy to tip from side to side to haul in a harpooned seal or salmon.

The shape of the boat resembled the figure of a recumbent man. "The nose is here," Axel said, pointing to the upturned wedge of the bow. "This stump here"—he indicated a round knot, several inches in diameter, poking up off the floor—"is the heart. It can be used to step a mast and put up a sail. Yurok sails were made from animal skins or woven from plant fibers. The boat could go upriver or out to sea. It was adaptable to both worlds."

Once he had finished carving, he intended to purify the boat with fire. Redwood chips would be placed inside and around the hull. The heat would temper the wood, while the smoke drove away bad spirits. In this manner, Axel would give back to the earth the power which he had appropriated to build the boat. After the fire cooled, friends and family would help launch the boat in nearby Trinidad Bay.

Axel spoke quietly, but with authority. His words were simple and precise. He paused to chuckle at something or to let what he had just said percolate through our brains. The flow of conversation kept our attention focused on the boat, rather than upon the skills that had gone into fashioning it. He told us that the little town of Trinidad Beach had once been the site of an ancient Yurok village known as Tsurai. He knew for a fact that his ancestors had lived there for at least five generations. Recent archaeological digs had unearthed evidence that the site had been occupied since the 1620s, some forty years after Sir Francis Drake had sailed along the coast in the *Golden Hind.*

"My grandmother was the last full medicine woman of the Tsurai branch of the Yurok," Axel declared. "She died in nineteen forty, when I was twenty, at the age of a hundred and four. She was a good medicine woman. She never hurt anyone. She used her power to help people. She could calm the sea by talking to it. She could send signals to birds. She could lure fish into nets by beating on seashells with a stick."

A brisk wind whipped in off the sea. The sky was clear, and the sun beamed brightly. It was mid-February, and a salty chill lingered in the air. The smell of the sea invaded my nostrils, making me light-headed.

It was my first visit to northern California. During the drive up from San Francisco, I had detoured off the main road to see the redwood trees. They were lofty trees, with runneled trunks of enormous girth supporting a vaulted canopy of branches and leaves. Little light filters down through the dense covering to the gloomy forest floor. The air was hushed, the silence broken by the squawking of an occasional jay.

Prior to European contact, Yurok Indians lived along this coast and along the banks of the rivers that wind down out of the foothills and empty into the sea. Back then the redwoods crowded up against the sea. Deer and elk and bear roamed freely. In the foothills flourished several varieties of oak, whose acorns provided an important source of food. Birds nested in staggering numbers in the marshes formed by rivers that poured into the sea. Salmon and steelhead trout surged back and forth between the ocean and their freshwater sources in complex migratory cycles.

Axel suggested that we go to his house and look at some old maps and photographs. Guy Mount, my companion, was especially pleased with the invitation. After moving to northern California several years ago to establish a bookstore and publishing operation, Guy had made a special trip to Trinidad Beach. He had some personal problems to sort out, and the beach radiated a mystique that he thought might be helpful. Again and again he came back to the little town to stroll along the bay and gaze out at the angular rocks, slick with spray, that rose through the surf. In that curious way that certain places have, it spoke to him and he responded. Though he couldn't define exactly why he, a native Ohioan, should be attracted to this far-off spot, he remained attentive. He sensed there were stories about the place that might help him lead a better life.

We drove down the road through a melancholy, late-morning light. Axel lived in a faded yellow frame house, on a quiet street near the cliff overlooking Trinidad Bay. Several vehicles, rusted and disused, were parked in the gravel driveway. Guy took one look at the ferns and mosses sprouting off the roof and smiled appreciatively. "This is an Indian house, all right," he muttered. "White people scrape the vegetation off their roofs."

We found ourselves in a spacious kitchen, softly lit by two high windows overlooking a tiny plot of grass. A sturdy table with thick legs occupied the center of the room. Axel brought out a portfolio of photos of Yurok elders, including one of his father taken in 1912 standing in rubber waders and holding a large halibut.

Another photo, dating from the turn of the century, showed two Yurok men, leathery and dark-skinned— their faces surprisingly smooth and fine-boned despite their advanced ages—standing in front of a sweathouse. One man had his arm around the shoulders of the other. "Soon after this photo was taken," said Axel, "the man on the right was dead. His friend died a few weeks later, reportedly of a broken heart."

I was attracted to Axel's voice. It was a light baritone, soothing and melodious. He spoke simply and directly, emphasizing the words with occasional gestures from his small, compact hands. There was something precise and correct about the way he spoke; he didn't falter or grope or overextend himself in his efforts to describe the contents of the photographs. Everything he said rang with authenticity. He spoke as effortlessly as the wind that swept over the house.

He was eager to tell the story of his grandmother, who had passed on to him much of the lore and knowledge she had accumulated as a medicine woman. "I know many of her songs and stories," he confessed. "Some of them are so powerful that I will never reveal them. But I would like people to know more about her."

There was a photograph of her sitting with another woman on the back steps of a house, squinting into the sun. It had been taken sometime in the 1920s. The woman had cropped white hair and a cherubic face. Her eyes, slotted against the glare of the sun, were creased and unfocused; her jowly cheeks looked plump and relaxed. There was something benign and appealing about her expression that the grainy texture of the photo couldn't entirely conceal. She wore a plain dress; over her shoulders was draped a light-colored sweater. Other than the unmistakable Oriental-Indian face, her clothes and bearing—including the gentle countenance radiating from her eyes—were similar to those of my own German grandmother back in Missouri. At one time in America all grandmothers, whatever their ethnic heritage, must have looked like this, tender and well-fed.

"A few years ago, down in San Francisco, I had open-heart surgery," Axel said. "And, do you know, something happened the day before I went under the knife that said I'd come out okay. It was as if the spirit of my grandmother appeared to let me know I'd pull through all right. I was sitting in a chair by the window of my hospital room when I heard a loud thump. A bird had knocked itself against the glass. I watched as it fell to the street below, frantically beating its wings.

"Well, a miracle happened. Instead of hitting the pavement, it got its wings going again and pretty soon it flew back up just as high as it had been. When it swooped by my window I let out a little cry. I knew then that I was going to survive the surgery the next day. The bird had given me a clear signal. I knew that I was every bit as tough as that little bird."

Axel paused. A slow smile like a smear of delicious honey spread across his face. For a moment he seemed to look deep into himself, toward a secret center; then, as if acknowledging something he liked, his face brightened and his dark eyes reflected a light that seemed to radiate from that center.

There were other photos in the collection, of men in traditional costumes and women wearing woven skull caps and shaggy maple-bark skirts. There was also an intriguing photo of the old village of Tsurai, taken sometime in the last century. It was splotchy and underexposed; the plate seemed to have been smudged during the developing process. Apparently the photo had been taken not far from the spot where Axel's house now stood; the view was similar to what we

42

had seen driving along the street above the cliff. In the foreground was an array of primitive shacks; in the background, poking out through the water, were the splintered sea stacks. The uneven rendering—clear in places, murky in others—was strangely compelling, like certain dreams that are exact in some details and confusing in others.

The traditional center of the Yurok universe was located farther up the coast, near the mouth of the Klamath River. From what Axel revealed to me, I got the impression that the Yurok world was hermetic and circumscribed, like certain features of California society today. The Yurok viewed the earth as wide and flat, traversable by a man in a redwood canoe. It was bounded at one end by an upriver ocean and at the other by a downriver ocean. Maintaining the earth on a level keel so that it wasn't flooded by the waters of either ocean was the primary task of the Yurok religion. This delicate equilibrium could be maintained only through periodic rituals, including a vigorous dance in which all the villagers participated, the main purpose of which was to keep the earth properly balanced so that it wouldn't tip too far in one direction or the other. With the decline of the Yurok in the twentieth century, there are not enough feet to settle the earth during the dances, with the result that the world has become tipsy and unstable, in danger of being inundated by both oceans.

Inside the tidy kitchen the air was hushed and still. Through the window I could see the diminutive yard and the pigeon-gray asphalt of the empty street. The atmosphere inside the high-ceilinged room was pleasantly drowsy. Axel's children had grown up and moved away; a few photos were the only reminders that these walls and floors had once resounded with the clamor of family voices. The room reminded me of a cheerily illuminated vault, redolent with personal and ancestral memories. I felt that if I sat here long enough, the lineaments of another world—similar to my own in many respects, vastly different in others—would reveal themselves.

The kitchen reminded me of my grandmother's kitchen in the stately house where she had lived for the last three decades of her life and where I used to spend a lot of time as a boy, watching her putter from stove to sink to refrigerator, whistling raspily between her strong white teeth. She couldn't calm the sea with her voice or persuade fish to give themselves up for food, but she had her own stories to tell in an indolent Missouri accent that rose and fell as effortlessly as water in a creekbed. How easy and pleasing her voice sounded in person, and how tinny and constricted over the telephone, whenever she called to speak to my mother.

It was Axel's voice that now transported me back to the past I remembered so well, an intimate past that, even while I relived it, seemed to enlarge to include particulars from Axel's own life, as he remembered it. It was like sitting down with someone at a table laden with good food and trading back and forth, a chunk of warm bread for a slice of dripping beef, a crisp vegetable for a ripe fruit, until all hunger was satisfied.

The night his grandmother died in 1940 he was sleeping in the room next to hers. The old woman had been failing for several days, and family members had taken turns sitting up with her. "I will let you know when I leave," she had whispered to him.

Exhausted by the vigil, Axel had fallen asleep, only to be awakened by the sound of someone shuffling along the hallway, bumping against the wall. It was a game that his grandmother had played with him when he was a boy; she had never passed the door to his room without giving a signal. Axel's mother heard the sounds, too, and rolled out of bed to check on the old lady. When Axel entered the room a moment later, his grandmother's round face was pointed sightlessly at the ceiling, the features composed in a mask of peaceful resignation.

The three of us sat for a while, absorbed in the story, smiling quietly to ourselves. The wind made a noise across the roof like the whisk of a giant broom. My imagination was transported outside the walls to the beach on the other side of the road. Perhaps my ears were playing tricks, but I thought I could hear the surf raging past the rocks offshore, the same rocks so starkly depicted in the photo Axel had shown us, lean and moss-backed and oddly menacing.

These rocks must have been appealed to again and again by all kinds of people. Guy had prayed to them for strength and counsel; no doubt Axel's grandmother, and even Axel himself, had done the same. I wondered what endows certain features with power. A combination of sunlight and water? The peculiar configuration that weathering can produce? The transmogrification of animal spirits into stone?

Different shapes awaken different responses. One of the enduring appeals of landscape lies in the longing for harmony and integration it evokes inside us. In a curious way these rocks seemed to be willful embodiments of an innate desire to locate insight and understanding in the features of natural objects. I couldn't help admiring any belief that rooted itself in a particular topography. How satisfying it must be to look out the window, in all kinds of weather, and observe the primal evidence of one's faith.

Axel's gentle voice shook me from my reverie. He was telling another story. One spring day in 1945—he was precise about the year—two teenage Yurok girls

45

were walking on the beach at the foot of the cliff. "They saw a woman," he said, "sitting on a rock. They thought they recognized her and called out her name. When they got closer they realized that it was someone else. The woman had dark skin. She was sitting there without a stitch of clothing. Her long hair fell over her chest and legs like strands of kelp. She stared at the girls with a piercing expression. She wasn't hostile or unfriendly. There was something strange and unearthly about her.

"Slowly the girls began to back away. They knew who she was and the sight of her made them tremble. They gasped when the woman stood up and, with her long hair cascading about her body, walked unhurriedly into the water and swam out to the rocks and disappeared."

Guy stared at Axel.

"It was the last time she was ever seen on this beach," the old man added.

"Ocean Lady," Guy whispered as if in shock.

"That is correct. You know her, too?"

"I wrote about her once. I caught the story on one of my first trips here to the beach." His face glowed with the excitement of an unexpected discovery. "I can't believe I'm hearing about it now, here in this place."

"Has she been seen anywhere else since then?" I asked.

Axel nodded. "But a long way out from here, far out in the ocean or in remote sections along the coast. Today, there are too many people on this beach. Too many houses and cars. Ocean Lady is leery of them. She's taken herself off to other places."

The air inside the high-ceilinged room was perfectly still. The light filtering through the windows was bright and clear, illumining the tiniest details on the

46

walls. Axel sat in a straight-backed chair, both feet planted squarely upon the wood-plank floor, his hands clasped in a loose knot over his lap. As his head tipped forward, his nut-colored jowls bunched in wrinkly folds against his neck. Guy stared out the window, absorbed in his own thoughts. That's how it once was, I concluded to myself. The earth does emanate real magic, and this man and his people have been witnesses to it. All the unpleasant thoughts, the cynical ravings, the furious outrage against contemporary life, abated momentarily on a swell of contentment. The world seemed as unified and self-contained and comprehensible as the Yurok Indians had once perceived it to be.

Axel scuffed his feet almost apologetically. "You can catch a song," he whispered, "by listening to the sound of water as it rushes past the bow of a canoe. You can. I've done it myself."

A few minutes later we said our goodbyes. Axel's handshake was firm and resolute. At the door he told a little joke that made us laugh. Guy made arrangements to meet with him again. I reached out and touched the fleshy part of his upper arm, uttered another goodbye, and walked out to the car with Guy. The gravel crunched pleasantly under our feet. The smell of brine from the sea filled my nostrils with a tangy scent. "I think I know why I was always attracted to this beach," Guy said as he opened the car door. He looked back thoughtfully at the house. "It's because Axel has helped preserve the mystery of the place with his stories. He's the guardian, the caretaker. As long as he's here he'll keep things right."

The car edged around a corner, and suddenly we had a panoramic view of the beach from the same perspective as the old photo of the village of Tsurai that Axel had shared with us. Below the road a rounded headland rose out of the water; curving toward the south in a crescent arc, backed by a steep cliff, was the pebbly, kelp-strewn margin of Trinidad Beach. Out in the surf, sparkling in the bright sun, loomed the splintered rocks. A delicate mist fanned off the wavetops, through which the rocks glimmered like a herd of charging horses. I hadn't felt this good in a long time. The burden of my life—the annoyances and sorrows, anxieties and grief—seemed to slip from my shoulders like a cape. I felt young again, feisty and indomitable. Guy suggested we get some lunch, and I nodded eagerly.

The Return of Beaver
to the Missouri River

In an autobiographical volume entitled *The River and I*, John Neihardt recounts the first time he ever looked upon the Missouri River. It was sometime in the late 1880s, and the place was Kansas City. The river was in full flood, a "yellow swirl that spread out into the wooded bottomlands," demolishing entire towns. "There was a dreadful fascination about it," Neihardt remembers, "the fascination of all huge and irresistable things. I had caught my first wee glimpse into the infinite. . . ."

Some seventy years later, in the spring of 1953, I stood on a bluff in St. Joseph, Missouri, and watched the last great flood of that unruly river ravage the bottomlands between my home town and the hills of distant Kansas. Augmented by several weeks of ferocious rains, tributaries in Iowa and Nebraska had disgorged an unprecedented volume of water into the Missouri, which quickly overflowed its banks. Levees crumbled, dikes collapsed, water swept across wheat and alfalfa fields, carrying houses, cattle, barns, and automobiles with it. From bluff to bluff between the two states, a distance of maybe five miles, the river was stippled with foamy whirlpools and entire trees. I remember watching the procession in stunned silence with my father and his friends. All my life (I was then twelve) I had heard of the river and watched it from passing cars and trains and even viewed it once or twice from airplanes, but I had never been on it in a boat or (God forbid) swum in it. That was unthinkable. The river was too capricious to attempt such a feat. There were boiling eddies that could devour the strongest swimmer, deadly snags and sawyers that could rip open the stoutest hull, animals with pointy teeth that could tear off a leg or arm. No, the river was a creature to observe from a distance and to cross as quickly as possible; it was not a place to linger in idle contemplation or recreational enjoyment. It was an unbridled monster in dire need of hobbling.

"That sure is a hell of a lot of water," remarked one of my father's friends.

"The airport's gone. Elwood's under water. A few feet more and it will wash over the Pony Express Bridge," said another.

"Yeah, but this won't keep up for long," declared a third. "Once they close off those dams up in Dakota, this ole river's gonna get trimmed down to size."

I think of that exchange now, thirty years later, whenever I launch my raft or canoe out on the river. Within the scope of a few decades it has changed in character and shape. It no longer is as wide as it once was; neither does it flood as torrentially. Periodically, it spills over its banks and inundates the lowlands, but it no longer rolls from bluff to bluff or sweeps through entire communities, stranding people in trees. Rarely does it bring the media rushing to its cresting banks. The dams up in South Dakota and the Army Corps of Engineers have taken care of that. Over the years the Corps has deepened the channel and made it more accessible to barge traffic. More recently, the Corps has lined the banks with a solid wall of riprap and installed wingdikes which jut out into the water at right angles; silt, building up behind these protrusions, progressively narrows the river's width. Gradually, the Corps has exerted more and more control over the river, reducing it in size to a tawny ribbon whose least impulse can be carefully monitored. In the process commercial fishing has become almost nonexistent, and the meandering oxbows—remnants of the river's earlier path— have dried up, drastically reducing the acreage of precious wetlands, prime nesting places for waterfowl.

"You know what that river has become?" a man said to me recently in a bar in Kansas City. "An irrigation ditch, that's what. A goddamn irrigation ditch!"

He had grown up in St. Joseph in the 1920s and '30s, and had fished on the river as a boy. Once, on his sixteenth birthday, he had swum the width, from Kansas back to the Missouri side. When he told me that, I gazed at him with speechless admiration. When I was growing up, swimming the river was the most daring thing a boy could do, more daring than stealing the old man's car for a joyride or crawling through sewer pipes under a cemetery or putting your hand on a girl's breast or even engaging in BB-gun wars.

Despite considerable changes that have severely modified its character, the river is still regarded with trepidation by most people who live near it. The reasons for this are mystifying. Recently, as I was tying my canoe on top of my car, my neighbor—an amiable man in his sixties, a veteran of the Battle of the Bulge—strolled over to help me adjust the ropes and tie the knots. "Where you headed?" he asked after pronouncing the boat secure.

"I'm going on the river."

"The Missouri!"

"Yep. A day float down from the mouth of the Platte."

He pulled carefully on his cigarette. "Well, you want to think twice before doing that, don't you?"

"Why?"

"It's dangerous. There're whirlpools that can easily upset a canoe the size of yours."

"Have you ever been on the river?" I asked.

"No. But I grew up around here, and I know when to stay away from a place that doesn't want me."

As I drove to the river I thought about what he had said. He had encouraged me to enjoy an outing on Smithville Lake, a reservoir located northeast of Kansas City, filled with power boats and water skiers and beer-drinking people swaddled with layers of fat. Their presence aside, there's something about still water that doesn't engage my imagination the way moving water does. A river flows from point to point and around the next bend; scenes unfold in slow procession with subtle variations. The sense of motion is invigorating.

My neighbor's remarks recalled the look of incredulity on my father's face the first time I told him I was going on the river. I might just as well have put a gun to my head and pulled the trigger, he declared, for all the chance I had of surviving.

"But you don't understand," I protested. "The river has changed since the time you took me up on the bluff to watch the flood. You can still die there, I grant you. But it's not the power it once was."

"You're crazy," he concluded with a shake of the head. "You're crazy to tempt fate that way."

52

When the reality alters, the rhetoric seems to harden into place. At least that's what I concluded after talking with my father and neighbor—two men of the same generation and similar backgrounds and experiences. The Missouri River—the lower portion of it at least, from Gavin's Point Dam in South Dakota to its juncture with the Mississippi—is but a slip of its former brawly self; nonetheless, the popular perception of it remains the same. The folklore of the river still evokes images of greedy whirlpools and menacing trees and aquatic carnivores. Elements of these images persist, though in sadly reduced form. Added to these fears, of course, is the relatively new one of pollution, though like many rivers in the United States the Missouri is less contaminated now than it was twenty-five years ago, primarily because the stockyards of Omaha, St. Joseph, and Kansas City no longer pump their refuse directly into it. But the rhetoric persists, almost as if people need to believe all the bad things they've heard. The river is still configured in the local imagination—and not just by people my father's age—as an excess in need of correcting.

The fact of the matter is that the Missouri has been "corrected"—overcorrected to a fault, I would say: dammed, diked, dredged, and drained to suit the needs of the dying barge traffic industry—so it will no longer flood valuable property along the banks; so it will no longer serve as a breeding ground for superfluous fish and wildlife. Certainly as a cultural and recreational resource it has been sadly ignored. In Kansas City, for example, there is virtually no access to the river within the city limits; there is no museum or park along the banks where the river can be viewed and appreciated. Memories of the devastating 1951 flood are still vivid here; while that kind of destruction will never occur again, does it really make sense to construct more wingdikes and drain more oxbows and lay down more

53

riprap so that, within the city boundaries at least, the river will purl harmlessly as water through a sluice?

Enough water flows past Kansas City in a single day to satisfy its needs for an entire year. When I tell this to my river-running friends in New Mexico and the arid Southwest, they express envy and delight. But when they actually view the river and see the wing-dikes with the sandbars filling in behind them and the miles of concrete chunks lining the banks, they shrug and turn away. The river isn't very interesting, they seem to say. It isn't very wild.

And yet parts of it still are. You have to search for them, but they are there. Great blue herons still poke for frogs along the banks. Kingfishers rattle noisily between the trees. Borne by sultry thermals, turkey vultures hover over the bottomlands, scouting for carrion. Fish erupt from the scuddy current in flashes of sun-dappled scales. And the river still churns along its ancient bed, down from the Dakotas, across the loamy, fertile midsection of the continent, to its fabled confluence with the Mississippi. Always, even in its present denatured form, there is a sense of movement, of process, of rhythm . . . of a metabolism older and wiser and more meaningful than anything yet invented by human ingenuity.

Historically, the Missouri River has defined one segment of the progressive western border of the American continent. It provided the pathway into the heart of the northern plains and brought trappers and explorers to the verge of the Rockies. In states like the two Dakotas it marks the boundary between one form of terrain and another. East of the river, the land is sectioned into small undulating farms with a distinct Midwestern feel; west of it, the grass diminishes in height, the range opens up to the horizon, and the sky arches endlessly like a yawning mouth. When the Teton Sioux first crossed the river in significant numbers in the mid-eighteenth century, their culture changed dramatically. For decades in southwest Minnesota they had been a woodland community, dwelling in deep pine forests, hunting and fishing on lakes, content with occasional forays onto the plains. Once they crossed the river their transformation into a fierce warrior society, the most respected of all Plains Indians, was assured. Armed with French rifles and mounted on Spanish horses, they created, through legendary heroes like Crazy Horse and Sitting Bull, a reputation for valor that endures to this day. Ahead of them lay the Badlands and the Black Hills and battlefields like the Rosebud and the Little Big Horn. Behind them, frothy and unpredictable—a Rubicon of the sensibility that forever distinguishes the western imagination from all others on the continent—flowed the massive, untidy, indefatigable Missouri.

Unquestionably, George Caleb Bingham was the premier artist of the Missouri River, if not the entire border region, and in the Metropolitan Museum of Art in New York City hangs one of his finest works, "Fur Traders Descending the Missouri." It depicts a man, probably of French extraction, and a boy, most likely a half-breed, sitting in a pirogue laden with furs. The time is early evening; roseate tints from the descending sun tinge the river's placid face and the trees in the background. The man smokes a pipe and dips his paddle in the water, more to steer than to accelerate the pirogue's speed. The boy leans against a hide-covered chest and stares dreamily into the artist's eyes. On the bow, tethered by a short rope, sits one of the most enigmatic figures in all of American painting . . . a dark, bristly, wolfish-looking animal with pointed ears and a glistening snout that appears to be looking down at its reflected image in the water—or is it staring into the artist's eyes?

Blake's tyger holds less portent for me than this

creature. I like to think that, intentionally or not, Bingham captured in this curious figure the true feeling of wilderness that the Missouri River once held for explorers and adventurers. That feeling has been described accurately and at great length by observers from Lewis and Clark to John Neihardt and James Willard Schultz; but no where else for me in all the art and writing produced by the region does it exist so powerfully. Whenever I bemoan the loss of the river's freedom, I look at that painting and am content that Bingham at least was able to capture a portion of what it once was and to pass it on for others to savor. Whenever I paddle my canoe on the silty current, I imagine the animal sitting in the bow, staring back at me with all the irony and inscrutability that two hundred years of bitter history can produce.

The Midwest is a sadly misunderstood place, routinely dismissed by Californians and Atlantic seaboarders, scorned by Rocky Mountain enthusiasts, and grudgingly defended by its own inhabitants. In a culture that celebrates spectacular surfaces, such a quiet, unruffled landscape is easy to ridicule. "I don't like to go west of the Alleghenies," a lawyer in New York once told me when I was a student there. "Missouri, Kansas . . . places like that. It's the same old thing, over and over and over again."

But it's not. The rivers of southern Missouri differ from the rivers of eastern Kansas. The foliage along the banks, the soil composition, the fish and animals vary in subtle, yet significant, ways. A sensitivity to the nuances of topography sharpens the eye and instructs the mind in the difficult task of making distinctions between organic forms. There is a moral here. The way we perceive landscape can have a direct bearing upon the way we perceive society and the human beings who comprise it. Dismissing a landscape because it does not conform to preconceptions is a prejudice as galling as dismissing people because of the color of their skin or the beliefs they profess. It violates the biological urge toward multiplicity and diversity that energizes our planet. By adjusting the rhetoric of perception to the reality of the fact perceived—by making the two more consonant and therefore truthful—our sensibilities can be sharpened and refined, and wherever we go in the world, instead of adopting the prevailing stereotype, we can encounter the reality, the genuine forms, that reside underneath.

One evening, after floating all day down from Atchison, Kansas, a friend and I passed under the Leavenworth bridge just as the sun was about to set. Our destination was Parkville, Missouri, a small town a few miles upriver from Kansas City. The time was late summer; a full moon was due to appear in about an hour, and despite the obvious dangers of floating at night, we intended to do just that, guided by the moonlight and the phosphorescent markers on the channel buoys. Barge traffic had been light that day, but we needed to be wary of the occasional tree limb that bobbed just under the surface.

The moon, huge and full, came up over the trees on the east bank. The light spilled onto the leaves and spread in a wavering beam across the water. We watched with fascination as the sky and river seemed to swell under the eerie light. On the west bank, willows and cottonwoods stood out in bold relief; between them, dark and moist as the entrance of a cave, the shadows were alive with sounds.

Suddenly, closeby, there was a loud crash as if a rock had been chucked into the river, followed by another and another, echoing back and forth and far downstream. "What the hell was that?" my friend exclaimed; and I confess that at that moment images of river demons, passed on to me by another generation, surfaced in my brain. A moment later I saw a creature with a sleek head and flat tail slip off the bank and disappear into the water. "Beaver," I muttered, almost in disbelief. One of the stories I had heard as a boy was that the beaver had been trapped out in these parts, along with the otter and mink, leaving only the muskrat, a durable species.

Additional explosions sounded up and down the channel, signaling our presence. "Beaver," I whispered, and suddenly I had a vision of the river as it once was—wide, tumultuous, shoally with islands, teeming with birds and fish and animals. If this were 1832, their pelts would fetch hard silver down in Westport or in the trading posts of Blacksnake Hills. But it wasn't; that era, with its magnificent vistas and murderous events, was over. The future stretched before us with the same chimerical uncertainty as the river's path in the moonlight. Tonight we were just drifting along, enjoying the sights, the steady current, the moist air that lapped against our cheeks. As if in acknowledgment, more beaver boomed their warning signal. We laughed and called out to them. This time, I thought, we'll share the river together.

The Body
of the Island

Tacked to the kitchen wall of the field station, over a rickety bookcase of paperback bestsellers, was a map of Santa Cruz Island. The various elevations were marked, the prominent features, the major bays and inlets; brightly marked also, in contrasting colors, were the different faunal regions—pine trees high up on the ridges, live oaks and chaparral on the slopes, willows and fennels in the washes that sluice down to the sea.

But most interesting of all was the outline of the island, its peculiar shape. Like some kind of unclassified fish, I thought, with a thickset body, truncated tail, a knobby neck that widened into a squarish head, and a bulbous point at the eastern tip reminiscent of the famous nose of Charles de Gaulle.

From the heights of Santa Barbara on the mainland I had observed the shadowy profile of the island through a veil of summer haze, but I didn't see it with any clarity until we were barely a mile from the wooden cattle pier that juts out into the cold, blue water of Prisoners' Harbor on the island's north side. The ride in the Navy boat from Port Hueneme across Santa Barbara Channel was rough and uneasy, and for the entire two hours I sat very still on deck with my eyes half-closed, breathing between clenched teeth, praying I wouldn't get sick. In the lee of the harbor the water calmed down, the boat stopped pitching, and I staggered to my feet. The view was impressive. Massive hills, grooved and rounded, their smooth slopes glowing in the midday sun, rose out of the sea like the tawny bodies of basking sea lions. Along the beach and down in the draws that cut through the hills grew stands of dark green trees. The wind that luffed across the harbor brought to my nose the licorice scent of sun-drenched fennels.

A truck transported us up the bumpy road, crossing and recrossing the pebbly bed of a stream, into the spacious width of the central valley. Nestled under a colonnade of eucalyptus trees was the field station where visiting researchers stay. There are no paved roads on Santa Cruz; dirt tracks radiate from the valley that splits the island like a seam, up and over the steep hills and coastal ridges, down to the sea. There are few electronic devices on the island, few television sets, and even fewer telephones. Thanks to the Stanton family, which for fifty years operated the island as a cattle ranch, and the Nature Conservancy, which in the future intends to restore the fauna to its original condition, Santa Cruz has miraculously escaped the impact of development that has blighted so much of mainland California.

60

After stowing our gear in our quarters, Ralph Cleven-
ger and I gassed up the jeep that had been put at our
disposal and chugged off to explore the eastern end of
the island. From the mouth of the stream that trickles
into Prisoners' Harbor the road winds up a succession
of sere hills toward the ridge that dominates the neck
of the island. The afternoon was flawless. A warm sun
beat down; a stiff wind rippled the dry, golden grass
that spread out over the hills and that for a hundred
years had provided ample fodder for grazing animals.
After climbing a few hundred feet, we got a fine view
of the channel separating Santa Cruz and the mainland; a wall of shiny mist was drifting down the channel from the northwest. "By this evening that fog will
curl around the island like a cat and poke up into the
draws and washes," Ralph said. "You watch. It'll lap
over into the central valley and before midnight fill it
up like ice cream in a bowl."

With Ralph at the wheel we drove along the wide,
graded road toward the Naval Radar Station, which
bristled with discs and antennae at the top of the ridge
like some kind of obscene fungus. The hills fell sharply
away from the road as we mounted higher toward the
apex. A brisk wind swept over the slopes, stirring the
grass in shimmering bands. Live oaks glistened in oily
clusters in the hollows and draws; the satiny red bark
of gnarled chaparral glimmered between the trunks.
The air was alive with birds. Doves arced over the hillsides as if catapulted from slingshots. A redtailed hawk
hovered over a patch of grass. Huge ravens, croaking
magisterially, lumbered into the wind like tar-coated
cargo planes.

Past the radar station the road abruptly narrowed.
We were on the neck of the island now, puttering
along the heights of a line of lofty hills that stretched
east toward the Gherini property, consisting of some

six thousand acres, owned by descendents of Justinian Caire, an early settler. The view from this vantage point of both the Pacific and the Santa Barbara Channel was splendid. The Pacific side was smooth, the water extending in a crinkly expanse out to a smudgy white horizon. Down the channel from the northwest rolled an impressive wall of mist, which by evening, as Ralph had predicted, would envelop the island, penetrating to the depths of the central valley. The boxy silhouettes of container ships were visible far out in the channel.

Periodically Ralph stopped the jeep, took out his camera and tripod, and went off somewhere to photograph a plant or tree. The hillsides were latticed with sheep and feral pig trails; the former followed the contours in a succession of concentric bands, while the latter shot up the sides in more or less straight lines. The cattle that once grazed the slopes everywhere on the island are gone, as are most of the sheep; feral pigs remain in considerable numbers, tough little porkers, sinewy and lean. Both sheep and pigs were introduced in the 1850s; the absence of predatory animals like wolves and bears made the place ideal for stock raising. The mild climate fostered year-round foraging; there was no deep snow to bury the grass, and the live oaks produced an ample supply of acorns.

By late afternoon a smooth, interlocking pattern of dark shadows was stealing up the slopes out of the gullies and ravines. (Night seems not only to descend from above but to creep up out of the earth.) I jotted down a few notes, but there was too much to see and absorb; while Ralph photographed the plants and grasses, I tramped away from the road. The ridge, broken into a jumble of rounded hills and cascading gullies, was difficult to traverse on foot. I wandered around awhile, inhaling the salt-laced air.

62

It was my first trip to Santa Cruz Island. Ralph *The Body* had been before; we were researching a book project *of the* that would take two years to complete. I can take two *Island* years of this, I thought as I lay back in the grass on a slope overlooking the road, overlooking another slope that pitched dizzily into a chaparral-tangled draw. (The angles at this elevation were acute and exposed; stretches of the road were so open to the light and air that I feared that a strong wind might catch the jeep like a kite and whisk it out to sea.) Two ravens passed overhead, the primary feathers of their glistening wings flexed apart like fingers. Gawky, cumbersome creatures, their presence always perked up a landscape. They hinted at a deeper attachment, the oblique perception, an imaginative crystalization of the particular and the arcane. One had to be careful with this bird; it was easy to convert from pure fact to mythological fancy.

A soothing warmth rose out of the hills like the heat from an oven. The island seemed a massive lump of sculpted dough, slowly baking to a golden-brown under the steady beam of the sun. I closed my eyes and stretched out my legs. The next thing I knew Ralph was calling up to me from the road. The leading edges of the fog bank had commenced to fold around the eastern end of the island, and the shadows stealing out of the draws and gulches were nearing the summits of the hills.

The next morning we climbed back into the jeep and puttered out toward the west end of the island. The road took us through a grove of towering eucalyptus trees that cast a gloomy shadow across the forest floor. (Introduced from Australia in the 1880s, the island's blue-gum eucalyptus are among the oldest and tallest in California.) We paused to listen to the peeling branches grind against one another, producing a fervent, deep-throated groan similar, as Ralph remarked, to the sounds that whales make underwater. The understory was littered with dried leaves and strips of bark. On down the valley we went, out into the sunlight where we surprised a pair of island fox. They regarded us shyly but inquisitively. About the size of a house cat, the fox is the largest indigenous animal on the island. It lives in burrows and ravines, and forages boldly in daylight. Its chest, legs, and underbelly are colored a bright rust, its back and face a bluish gray.

We then climbed a steep incline to a narrow valley boxed in on both sides by live oaks; high up on a rounded saddle spanning the coastal ridges we were greeted by a refreshing whiff of salt air. From the saddle the road snaked down a narrow defile splashed with Mariposa lilies, which Ralph paused to photograph. The south coastal ridge was almost entirely covered with bishop pines, while the foothills to the north, continually exposed to the sun, remained rocky and treeless. The road at this point was little more than a two-wheel track, precariously steep in places, especially where it dipped down through deeply eroded washes. The defile eventually widened into a lateral valley that funneled like a chute toward the sea. Lush meadows unfolded to either side; meadowlarks trilled in the grass. A short time later we rumbled past a primitive airstrip and arrived at the gate of Christy Ranch, where the road branched off toward Forney's Cove near the truncated tail of the island. The time was 12:30. This little ramble of approximately ten miles had taken us nearly three hours. Through a scrim of haze, Santa Rosa Island came into view on the other side of a narrow strait. The landscape at the west end shelved down to the water in a series of treeless, windswept terraces that at one time had been part of the ocean floor. Forney's Cove was a scenic inlet with a shingled beach littered with strands of shattered kelp. We stopped the jeep and brought out lunch, and, while Ralph photographed various plants and rocks, I strolled along the sand skipping stones out over the creamy wavetops.

On the return trip to the field station we followed a trail that looped up and down over the contour of the south coastal ridge. Ironwood trees grew in formidable stands that bristled up from the hollows and depressions marking the slopes that in turn fell away toward the central valley. The exposed soil was a vivid Ozark red, so different from the muted earth tones of the lower reaches. We had a marvelous view of the valley, the eucalyptus grove, the whitewashed planks of the field station, the wide fault line that threads the valley floor. The jeep hitched along at barely ten miles an hour, enabling us to absorb all the views in a leisurely fashion, letting our eyes linger on any scene for as long as we wanted. It occurred to me then that the best way to become acquainted with a landscape is to crawl across it on your belly. Details unobservable from a standing position will disclose themselves, and like a lizard—or, better still, a gliding snake—you register upon your sensitive belly plates a variety of textures and temperatures. You process information through the digestive capacity of the abdomen, rather than piecemeal through the senses. The experience of the terrain enters your body in the form of a solid charge that spreads without resistance to every extremity.

By the end of the second day on Santa Cruz Island, my head was swollen with images of the colorful hills and expansive sky. At supper I ate slowly and ruminatively.

Ralph and I discussed what we had seen so far and what still needed to be done. Despite our enthusiasm, a significant portion of our communication remained unspoken, a deeper appreciation of the island and its attributes that, by tacit understanding, we were wary of touching upon.

That night while I slept, a mouse squeezed under the door of my little room in the field station, climbed up onto the bunk, and brazenly nibbled at the tips of my outstretched fingers. I awoke with a start, wheezing with panic. My heart clattered inside my chest like a squirrel in a metal cage. The mouse scurried off the bed, but I could hear it scuttling around the floor near my boots and smelly socks. "Bastard," I growled. My skin tingled as if it had been irritated by the oil of a noxious plant. It was some time before I was able to fall back to sleep.

We were up by five the next morning and off by jeep into the moist, fog-muffled dark. Ralph wanted to take some sunrise shots from the east end of the island. Sleep clung to our faces like sticky webs. Disconnected remnants of a puzzling dream floated through the ether of my brain. The air was brisk and cool, and we sat huddled in the vehicle wiping the moisture off our cheeks and glasses. Up the same well-graded road toward the radar station we bumped and rattled, through a glaucous pre-dawn light that every moment revealed more of the island's features. From the heights of the ridge overlooking the neck we could see layers of muffling fog that during the night had spilled over the coastal ridges and down into the central valley and along the declivities that branch off in random directions. The Santa Barbara Channel was socked in by a solid bank that appeared to be rolling our way; over its rumpled ceiling, twenty miles or more distant, rose the silhouette of the mainland mountains. To the south,

66

far out to sea, the fog was fashioned in a gothic array of shapes—patchy clouds, tufted bunches, twisted coils, gargoyle-like clumps—that seemed to sway and shimmy under pressure of an invisible hand. The wind from the mainland blew the channel fog onto the island, obscuring the turtle-backed ridges and hills. One moment the forms of the island were evident, and the next they were obscured.

Despite the appearance of the condensed shroud, I could feel the earth under my feet begin to stir sluggishly. The island was waking up and so were we. Ralph plunked down the tripod and fastened the camera to it. He was hoping that with the arrival of the sun the fog would lift and he could obtain a shot of the hilly east end, the pewtered surface of the water, the serpentine profile of Anacapa Island, which lies just behind Santa Cruz. Somewhere in the murk— close-by, to judge by the intensity of its croak—a raven wheeled and dipped. The fog was moving swiftly now, swirling up the hillsides and slipping over their crests. A pale, milky sun had finally pulled itself up over the horizon—not exactly what Ralph was looking for, but he clicked away boldly. As if excited by the milk-white sheets scurfing over the ridge, the invisible raven began to caw raucously.

And then, with eerie alacrity, the fog blew away and one by one the nearby hilltops swam into view, lifting through the murk like the backs of surfacing whales. The sun at 6:25 this June morning resembled a tarnished wafer clinging to a vertical plate, but within moments its character altered, the shape blurring as a sulphurous glow lit up its pallid face. "Definitely a summer sun," I muttered to Ralph. Springing up from the horizon purposefully and in earnest, with no hesitation or pussyfooting around. We heard the cheery trinkle of a meadowlark from somewhere down the hill.

The Chumash Indians, who once lived on this island, personified the Sun as a cranky, rapacious old man who each day circled the earth brandishing a torch. In the morning he carried the torch high, gradually lowering it as the day went on. During each circuit, prompted by hunger, Sun snatched up people and tucked them under his headband. At night in his fog-shrouded house he passed his victims through the torch two or three times and devoured them half-cooked, slaking his thirst with their blood.

With the sun now fully up, Ralph moved his tripod to the edge of a manzanita growth in hopes of capturing the image of a fox. The wind from the mainland had shoved the fog completely off the crown of the island. All the salient features of the topography were plainly exposed. In the expanding light, I realized that the ground was littered with cowpiles, crusty evidence of the huge herds that had recently roamed the hills and valleys. I kicked several aside and stretched out on my back. It seemed the best posture from which to view the ascent of the morning. I closed my eyes. Immediately, I heard a raven sawing through the air. Evidently he wanted to determine whether I was edible or not. The sun began to warm my face and arms. In a little while I would be peeling off my clothes to escape the heat. Back the raven came, closer this time, paddling no more than ten feet over my upturned face, peering at me through one beady eye. When I moved my legs he flapped away, obviously wanting no part of a breathing animal this morning.

And so it went, day after day, one marvelous sensation succeeding another, the images marking deep intaglios upon our consciousness, scoring impressions all the way to the bone. One afternoon we jolted over the south coastal ridge and down a willow-choked wash to a protected anchorage with a pair of sea stacks looming offshore. The stacks were fringed with the stalks of dried coreopsis, which blooms vividly with bright yellow blossoms in the spring. Pelicans and cormorants swooped around the rocks. A harbor seal popped its sleek, inquisitive head up through a raft of floating kelp. At the mouth of the wash, a few yards from the waves that curled against the stony beach, sprouted the pale, velvety blossoms of the bewitching datura.

One morning we crept into a stand of ironwood trees situated on a hillside where Ralph set up his camera for some close-up shots of the trunks and foliage. I sprawled between two roots and took out a book, then put down the book to watch a scrub jay approach cautiously, fluttering from limb to limb. Santa Cruz scrub jays are bigger than their mainland counterparts, a product of island gigantism, a phenomenon that enables certain species to grow larger as a result of less competitive pressure from similar types, plus the absence of predatory enemies. The jay swept up to a branch just behind Ralph. In the shadowy light its blue back and head glowed with undiminished luster. Without looking up, Ralph—who enjoys the peripheral vision of a pro basketball player—acknowledged its presence with a wave of the fingers. The jay peered over his shoulder, inquisitive, alert. Ralph peered through the camera, the bird watched Ralph, I watched the two of them. There was a connection in this little triad that in its own modest way was deeply satisfying.

One evening we stood on a high ridge and watched a luscious moon slip over the eastern ramparts of the island, casting a faint oriental light down into the central valley. Ralph clicked away, impervious to the hordes of mosquitoes swarming around his head. The sky to the west was flawlessly clear, infused with the tarnished glow from a vanished sun. Rising across the valley was the inky dome of Picacho Diablo, the

69

highest point (2,434 feet) on the island. A mockingbird gurgled melodiously. Bats flitted antically through the air. The plaintive cry of a peacock floated up from Stanton Ranch. It was as if the island had taken on a secretive, invisible life in the belly of the darkness that presently enfolded it. Everything was so perfectly contained in the dry, windless air that I felt as if I could detect the earth's roll around the hub of an invisible axis, far under my feet. My legs were like magnetic pylons receiving information from the depths of the hills, information that energized not just my brain (which, in the dark, seemed puny and attenuated), but every part of my body.

And so it went, hour after hour, day after day, time stretching out to unaccustomed lengths, providing the most leisurely arena for perception and reflection. The nervy, kinetic rhythms that normally governed my life seemed to fall away like electric coils, exposing a vulnerable core. A sense of the possibility of a true primordial awareness gradually stole over me, the promise of a lifetime of deliciously slow and gratifying sensations. A knowledge of the corpus of the island, its general shape and specific details, unfolded in my mind like a delicately patterned sheet of paper. Piece by piece, image by image, feeling by feeling—similar in delight to the knowledge a lover acquires from observing and touching the body of the beloved. It may very well be the most satisfying form of knowledge that any individual can acquire.

Thousands of years ago Santa Cruz and several other Channel Islands were conjoined in a vast superisland known as Santarosae. There is speculation that this island was once connected to the mainland. (Geologically, the Channel Islands are an extension of the Santa Monica Mountains that run east-west across the top of the Los Angeles Basin.) As if to underscore this scien-

70

tific theory, the Chumash Indians tell how their people first reached the mainland by crawling along a rainbow bridge that arched out from the summit of Picacho Di- ablo. Halfway across, the bridge dissolved, spilling people into the sea, where they turned into porpoises whose silvery bodies can be seen today, flashing above the surface as if still trying to gain the shore of the elusive mainland.

The last afternoon, after gassing up the jeep at the Stanton Ranch, I walked into one of the outbuildings to note the number of gallons on a clipboard. Ralph stayed outside, checking something under the hood. The room was spacious, walled with whitewashed planks; the sun beat down on the roof, heating the air inside, charging it with a heavy animal smell. I logged in the number and turned around. Spread across tables and sawhorses were several saddles and bridles, articles from the days, not too long before, when the ranch had been worked by a troop of Mexican cowboys. A mix of worn leather and horse sweat filled my nostrils. Everything was left as it once had been— bridles, saddles, bits, reins, quirts, stirrups, thongs, boots, spurs, blankets, even stiff brushes full of bristly horsehair—as if the cowboys had just stepped into the ranch house for a bite to eat. (Every morning, mounted on their horses, the rowels of their heavy spurs jingling in the air, they rode under the colonnade of eucalyptus trees past the field station to tend the cattle grazing on the slopes of the central valley.) I started back across the room and then paused, transfixed by a sudden memory that rose up through my brain like the shadow of an ancient fish.

On the outskirts of the Missouri town where I grew

up there was a farm owned by my father's best friend, whose son I used to play with regularly. The farm covered several hundred acres, and we had the run of it, exploring everywhere, on foot or horseback or by tractor; there was always some new adventure to pursue whenever I came out from town. But what sticks in my memory, and what came back to me now as I stood in that room full of pungent saddlery, was the image of the cavernous stable where the owner kept the few horses that still worked the farm in the 1940s. A murky corridor, stacked with bales of hay, led past several stalls to a pair of double doors at either end, wide enough for a horse-drawn wagon to squeeze through. Next to the stalls was an anteroom you stepped up to; it was small and cloistered, the dark paneled walls decorated with girlie calendars and blurry photographs. A rolltop desk and iron safe took up one side; the rest of the room was filled with saddles and bridles, which gave off a fleshy, aromatic scent. I remember inhaling the air deeply each time I entered, thinking how different the smell was from the smell of the elegant, well-appointed farm house (manor house might be more precise) that graced the premises a quarter-mile away. How thick and dense and clotted that smell was; how different from any of the odors that emanated from my own house and neighborhood in town. I loved that barn. I loved to prowl the straw-littered corridor and peer into the stalls and inhale the reek of urine-soaked hay, a dank, mysterious smell that always sent a shiver up my spine. Barn swallows swirled up and down in the sunbeams that slanted through the filthy windows. Rats gnawed gaping holes in the baseboards. Squirrels dashed frantically over the dilapidated roof. Every now and then a huge black snake was discovered coiled up in a corner or on a tractor seat.

The memory flooded my consciousness as I stood in

the outbuilding of the Stanton Ranch on Santa Cruz The Body
Island, thousands of miles from my home town in Mis- *of the*
souri. I tapped the fingers of my right hand reflectively *Island*
against my thigh. Islands have the power to evoke the
deepest reveries from the recesses of the mind. I stood
there mesmerized, enveloped in a film of memory,
projected back across the lapse of decades to a period
that meant absolutely nothing to anyone other than
myself. The intensity of the flashback seemed to iso-
late me at the same time it quickened the pace of my
feelings; it was as if the memory had transfigured me,
delineating my identity to a narrow personal focus
from which it could never really evolve. A flush of self-
pity swept over me; I felt bereft and forsaken, and yet
curiously enobled by the piquancy of the moment.
There was no escaping the past that marched in quick
lockstep with each new foray I made into the future.
Free will was a concept that belonged exclusively to
animals and creatures with no power of recall.

I heard my name being called from outside. Ralph
had started the jeep and was ready to go for one final
crawl across the body of the island before we had to
catch the boat back to Port Hueneme. The spell dissolved, and I stepped out into the light and blinked my
eyes. From the cool shadows cast by the ranch house,
a peacock cried mournfully against the mindless glare
of the sun.

Country
to Make You Weep

I was standing near the rim of the Badlands Wall,
facing west, watching the last rays of a feeble January
sun fade into the horizon, when I became aware of
something behind me. The Badlands were barren and
empty, encrusted with snow in the gullies and washes
that sliced through the wall, brown and drably sere in
the rounded humps of the ridges and low hills that
rose to the north. A gray light flared off the wintry terrain, thinning to a faint azure high in the sky. To my
left the wall dropped hundreds of feet to an ill-defined
valley, hacked and threaded with creek beds. Several
miles to the south, glowing in the fading light like the
dull back of a snake, lay the shallow width of the
White River, marking the boundary of the Pine Ridge
Indian Reservation. Somewhere in that direction, two

coyotes began to yip in bloodcurdling voices. Their wailing struck a melancholy chord deep inside my chest. The sound was the perfect accompaniment to the desolate scene . . . an eerie, piteous screel that sliced through the air like a knife.

On impulse I turned and there it was, a round, softly glowing moon rising into the sky. I was amazed at how big it was in the middle of winter. I had this odd notion that, because of the cold, it shrank in January and swelled in summer. But this particular evening it was as big as I had ever seen it . . . a tarnished orb, splotched and cratered, luminous and shiny. As if in response, the coyotes redoubled their howling.

Down in the valley the lights of the little town of Interior winked on one by one. I opened the car door and squeezed inside. The engine turned over with a reluctant cough. A storm was due later tonight, a real howler out of the Rockies, that would deluge South Dakota with snow. I had been to the store that afternoon and had stocked up on supplies in my little room in the rangers' quarters at Badlands National Park. But I wasn't ready to go back there just yet. I needed company. I pointed the car down the road toward Interior and the lights that glittered in the darkening air.

The only place open was a bar called Mike's. The café was closed, the filling station, the post office; the town's few inhabitants had retreated into their modest homes or vanished into the night. A single bulb glowed over the entrance to Mike's; inside, a line of tiny red Christmas lights over the mirror behind the bar mingled with several bulbs of dubious wattage to produce a lurid, cave-like glow. Two Indian men of indeterminate age sat at the bar, smoking cigarettes and sipping beer. Mike stood behind the bar, working a crossword puzzle with a pained expression on his face. He was in his mid-thirties, with a scraggly goatee and blond hair that spilled to his shoulders.

The interior was hushed and deadly still. A couple of booths along one wall were occupied. In the back, clustered around a pool table next to a dance floor, stood a half-dozen Indians. One with a cue in his hand had glossy black hair that dangled to his waist. Those observing the game offered little comment as the players sent the shiny balls caroming around the table and into the pockets with a loud thwock. A few mumbling voices were all that could be heard; the jukebox sat silently against the wall.

I bought a beer and carried it over to a table. I opened the afternoon edition of the Rapid City *Journal* and turned to the sports page. The beer tasted curiously metallic to my cold tongue. I needed something to chew, so I purchased a bag of pretzels and began eating them one by one.

"*Wasicu?*"

The voice was faint and hesitant. "*Wasicu?*" it came again.

I looked up. The woman's face over the top of the seat in front of me was round and puffy and badly wrinkled around the eyes. A wool cap covered her skull; wisps of hair curled over her ears and down her neck.

"Pardon?"

"Will you buy me a beer, *wasicu?*"

"A beer?" I looked at her and then down at the paper. The Lakers were on a rampage, having won eight straight games on the road. "Sure, sure." I stood up and went to the bar.

"Lady over there would like a beer," I said to Mike.

"You buying?"

"That's correct."

Mike popped open a Budweiser and took my dollar. "She's been here awhile," he remarked.

"Maybe she's lonely."

"I think it's more than that."

One of the pool players had advanced to the bar and stood there, waiting to be served. He looked past both Mike and me at the bottles lining the counter, his thick, fleshy face composed into an expressionless mask. I got out of his way and took the beer over to the table and handed it to the woman.

"Thank you," she said. "You're a nice man. Would you sit with me awhile?"

I hesitated then picked up my beer from the other table and slipped into the seat beside her. She wasn't alone. Another woman sat across from her with the fingers of her right hand curled around a whiskey glass. There was little ice in the glass and lots of amber-colored liquid.

"This is Mary. My name's LaDonna."

I nodded to both of them. Mary's face was square and jowly, but rather pretty. She wore hoop earrings, and her cheeks were smudged with a pink blush.

LaDonna's eyes, as dark as chokecherries, were wet with tears. I babbled a few pleasantries then lapsed into silence. Mary stared at me in a friendly manner, as if she had questions but for the moment was too shy to ask them.

"Do you know what happened to me today, *wasicu?*" LaDonna said.

"What's that?"

"My daughter died."

Her voice seemed to catch like the toe of a shoe on a rumpled carpet.

"I'm sorry to hear that."

"Yes. She died today. This morning, in fact."

Mary took a long swallow from her glass.

"She had this thing wrong with her heart, and they took her to the hospital in Pine Ridge, and the doctors told me they couldn't do anything for her so they just let her die."

78

"Goddamn doctors," Mary muttered.

"They told me there was nothing they could do. There was a hole in her heart where all the blood had leaked out. She died in the hospital before I could get there. All I saw was the sheet over her face."

"I . . . I'm sorry to hear that."

LaDonna took my hand and squeezed it with her long brown fingers. A film of tears coated her murky eyes. Her mouth, which once had been attractive, was stretched like the mouth of a fish after a hard fight with a hook.

"Goddamn doctors," Mary muttered again.

"There was nothing they could do?" I said.

"She'd gotten sick one other time," she explained, "but they wouldn't take her then. One morning in a snowstorm she came to my house in Porcupine and crawled into bed with me and said, 'Mama, I feel real bad. I think I'm gonna die.' I drove her down to Pine Ridge, and the doctor ran his fingers under her breasts and said she wasn't sick and ordered me to take her home. That was two weeks ago. She died this morning."

"Goddamn doctors," Mary growled. "This doctor was Indian too."

"What do you think of that, *wasicu?*" LaDonna said, crunching my fingers in her strong grasp. "Isn't that the saddest story you ever heard?"

"I'm sorry," I said feebly. "I'm just very sorry."

"I know you are, *wasicu*. I know you are." She drank from her glass and brushed her lips with the tips of her fingers. "Why are you here, *wasicu?* What are you doing in this cold country?"

"I'm a writer. I'm writing a little book about the Oglala Sioux for the park service."

"About me!" Her face brightened and a wan smile fluttered across her spoiled mouth.

"Well, about all of you. Your history and culture."

"And what are you going to say about us?"

"I'm not sure yet. That's what I'm here to find out."

Mary leaned across the table. "I bet you write more about Red Cloud and Crazy Horse than us," she declared.

"Why's that?"

"Because they're dead."

I looked over at Mike. He had put down the crossword puzzle and was staring out the window into the street. The moon had vanished. A raft of scowling clouds had moved over the Badlands like a shroud. It seemed to have grown a little gloomier inside the bar. The two men sitting on stools continued to gaze into the mirror or up at the ceiling. A pair of crutches leaned against the thigh of one man. He had a slim back and narrow hips, and from across the room he looked rather young, though I could have sworn when I first saw his face that he was old enough to be my grandfather. The other man, two stools away, exhaled a stream of cigarette smoke into his left palm and watched intently as the smoke broke into fragments and floated up to the ceiling.

LaDonna continued to cry. Her shoulders trembled and her chin sank to her chest. Mary reached out and stroked her wrist. LaDonna clutched my fingers in an iron grip. Her hand was coarse and grainy as the surface of an unplaned board.

"She's been doing this all day," Mary whispered.

"There's not much else she can do, I guess."

Mary stared at me intently. She leaned over her whiskey glass, pressing her breasts against the table edge. "*Wasicu*," she whispered, "if I give you my address, will you write me?"

"Sure. I'll write you."

She didn't have a purse, and the only paper I could

find was a matchbook cover. I had to remove my hand *Country*
from LaDonna's grasp to give Mary a pen. *to Make*

While Mary wrote, her face puckered into a tight *You Weep*
squint, I said to LaDonna, "How old was your
daughter?"

"Thirty-four."

"Did she have children?"

She held up four fingers then fumbled for my hand
again. Mary reached across the table and tucked the
matchbook cover into my shirt pocket. "Be sure and
write to me. Please. I like to hear from people from
other places."

"I will. I promise."

Soft animal sounds blubbered between LaDonna's
teeth. "*Wasicu*," she mumbled, "ask Mike to play some
music so we can dance. I need to dance."

"Okay. Sure." I stood up reluctantly and walked to
the bar. "Mike . . . uh . . . can we play the jukebox?
The lady over there would like to dance."

Mike pulled his gaze away from the dark window
and fixed it upon my face. His beady eyes were slotted
closely together over the bridge of a high arching
nose, which gave his blond features a pinched and
squinty expression.

"Nobody can dance here on weekdays until after
eight o'clock," he said tonelessly.

"Maybe just this once, hey? The woman's in bad
shape. She lost her daughter today."

He shrugged. The expression on his face was stony
and rigid. "I can't make any exceptions. That's the way
it is."

A slow anger burned through my throat. I wanted to
scream at him, but I didn't. I tramped back to the table
and told LaDonna. She stared down at her hands
which lay twitching in her lap like a pair of stricken
animals. Mary stuck a finger into her glass. "I thought

he'd be different," she sighed. "He's married to an Indian girl. If she were here, she'd let us dance."

I didn't feel like dancing. I wanted to go back to my
room at the park and sit quietly for a while and let
everything settle in my brain like sediments in a cloudy
pool. "I think I'd better go," I said.

LaDonna was reluctant to release my hand. Mary
looked at me glumly. As gently as possible I loosened
LaDonna's grip on my fingers. I stood up and endeavored to be brisk and business-like. I picked up the
newspaper from the other booth, folded it neatly, and
tucked it under my arm like a man about to enter a
crowded subway. "Goodbye," I called. Neither woman
looked at me. Mary ran a finger around the rim of her
empty glass. LaDonna squeezed both hands between
her thighs and leaned her head, swathed in the wool
cap, against the wall.

I stood at the bar for a moment, feeling stupid and
helpless. The same two men were still sitting there,
drinking and smoking. The others in the back continued to play pool, wordlessly, with little banter or
calls of encouragement. Still others watched, absorbed
in their thoughts, taking pulls from long-necked
bottles of beer, expelling streams of cigarette smoke
that drifted over the table in a blue cloud.

Snow was expected later tonight in Arctic force. We
would all be shut into our respective dens for the next
few days. All the road crews in western South Dakota
had been alerted.

I took a ten-dollar bill out of my pocket. "Mike,"
I said, "buy those two ladies over there whatever
they want."

I was reluctant to give him the money, though I
knew he would be scrupulous about it. He was the sort
of man who could identify every penny he had ever
earned.

82

He pulled the crisp bill over to his side of the bar. *Country*
"You're not sticking around?" *to Make*
"I'm tired. I've got a lot of work to do. Besides, *You Weep*
there's a storm coming in."
"Yeah. I heard that. It should be a whopper."
"Good night then."
"Good night."

Outside the temperature had dropped, and the air
had acquired a menacing edge. Thick clouds obscured
the moon. It was as if a gigantic lid had been clamped
down over the town, sealing the inhabitants under it.
As the car engine kicked over, I thought of an old man
I had once met in my hometown in Missouri. His
name was Ernie Uhlmer, and at the age of nineteen, in
1908, he had journeyed up to South Dakota in a covered wagon to homestead. Beginning with the Dawes
Act in 1887, and continuing for many years thereafter,
the federal government sought to break up the com-
munal holdings of the Oglala Sioux by forcing them to
become individual property holders and throwing the
excess plots open to sale to white speculators. It was
one of these plots near the Pine Ridge Reservation that
Ernie had attempted to homestead. He lasted less than
a year, through one wretched winter and into the
spring before selling the horse and dilapidated wagon,
boarding the train, and returning to Missouri. "Too
dang cold and desolate," he declared. "The winter
nearly killed me. The Indians can keep the place for all
I care. They're tougher than me, and besides the land
belongs to them. Only they know how to live on it,
though for the life of me I can't figure out how. It must
be magic. All I could think of that whole long miser-
able winter was the rich black soil of Missouri and how
easy it is to dig your fingers into."

The engine finally sputtered into action. I let out
the clutch, and the car eased down the empty street.

Despite the intense cold, with the heater blasting, I rolled down the window. The tires crunched against the hard dirt street. Tomorrow, the street and everything around it would be buried under a foot of snow. As the car chugged out of town I listened for the coyotes, and when I didn't hear them I rolled up the window and turned on the radio.

Flying to Exuma

> One of the miracles of the airplane
> is that it plunges a man directly into
> the heart of mystery.
>
> Antoine de Saint-Exupéry

The pilot of the two-engine Cessna wants more weight up front and asks me to sit beside him. I'm not fat, I console myself; I just look mature. I settle in, strap the belt across my lap, and watch as he manipulates the controls and murmurs into the microphone crooking out from his ear.

The eleven-passenger plane is packed with people bound for Great Exuma Island in the Bahamas. Dwarfed by gigantic jets taking off and landing, the little plane trembles at the head of the runway. With maximum power applied to the props, the pilot releases the brake, and down the tarmac we glide with tipsy, swallow-like ease, pulling away from the ground almost prematurely with an effortless lunge. I feel a mingled sense of relief and foreboding as we roar over Miami Beach and leave the mainland behind. The parent body. The conti-

85

nental mass. Ahead, there is nothing but azure water speckled with whitecaps and pleasure boats.

Toward the heart of the Bermuda Triangle we wing, the blades of the twin propellers biting through the air. The vibration stutters through my nostrils, jangles my sinuses, with quavery precision pierces the forefront of my brainpan and makes me sneeze. I sneeze again. I am extended beyond the limits of my skin by the thrust of this marvelous machine. I feel as if my face has sprouted a propeller, my arms have elongated into metal wings.

Bimini Island, the first outpost, swims into view at five thousand feet, resembling an inverted fishhook on a turquoise field. How strange and alluring the shapes of small islands, like pictographic blots upon a wall! The sea is dappled with arresting shapes. A porous cloud cover diffuses the glare of the morning sun. The flight is scheduled to last one hour and forty-five minutes. That's all right with me. It can take all day. We are aloft and breezing through the sky, heading south, angling toward the tropics. Toward sunlight and warmth. Toward blue water and a shimmering horizon. Toward the flap of palm fronds and the slop of crinkly waves against a crescent shore.

Southeast of Bimini the aqua belt of the Gulf Stream discolors to a brooding depth. The floor of the Bahamian archipelago rises and falls in an irregular pattern. Fish prowl the water with mindless ease. They are cleverly disguised to conceal their true identity. They hang, transparent and bodiless, like a line of invisible wash. You might hear them flapping, though by the time you located them, their teeth would already have shredded your face. From the air the color of the water is a chameleonic pattern of blues and greens that alters in value like the segments of a kaleidoscope. I can almost hear the pieces click and dissolve as they turn in rhythm with the earth's rotation.

86

The pilot fiddles with the controls, resets his radio Flying
frequency to pick up the Nassau tower. His movements to Exuma
are serene and purposeful. The offices of an Aviator
Monk. The concept has a certain appeal. The pilot sits
poised at the wheel in a state of watchful quiescence.
Attentive immobility. Alert torpor. The quintessential
late-twentieth-century body position. Cultivated in
theatres and automobiles, in front of TV sets. Slack and
reposed, langorous and detached . . . so different from
the propulsive lurch of nineteenth-century locomotion.
Think of Audubon crashing through the brush in
search of birds or Sir Richard Burton plowing through
the African green. Back then, the objective was clearly
defined. Life was a chronic search for trophies. The
Holy Grail was transmuted into a heron feather.
Searching for the source of a river was tantamount to a
crusade.

We are the practitioners of a luminous passivity. We
sit as if strapped to a dentist's chair, jaws agape, eyes
half-closed, exposing our anesthetized gums to the
routine probing of a drill. Our immobility triggers a
rush of conflicting images. We are more mentally animated than our forebears, but secretly we yearn for the
slow, unhurried pace that will transport us to the gates
of eternity. "People today seem so nervous to me,"
Harry Truman once remarked in an interview. Yes, indeed. A farm boy always feels uneasy in the presence
of jerky, unconnected movement. Fortunately, a key
requisite for a pilot is a certain phlegmatic disposition.
We don't want them too impulsive. We prefer that they
be steady and reliable. I remember once in Agadir listening to the Moroccan flight crew arguing in rooster-
shrill voices as the aircraft taxied for take-off. This
button! No, you dog-faced son of a whore, it's this
one, I tell you! This one!

Or so, in my anxiety, I interpreted the dialogue.
They might have been exchanging pleasantries, for all

87

I know. Their voices were pitched at a register that sent an oily spasm through my bowels. How I longed at that moment to hear the oaken drawl of an Anglo-Saxon voice! Instead my stomach turned to glue, and I was certain that I was about to die. Miraculously the plane lifted off without mishap.

The Cessna pilot is young, thirty or thirty-five. He has an athletic face and sports a mustache. He wears Vaurnet sunglasses, which give him a debonair look. He seems to know what he's doing; his movements are deft and economical. He takes time to answer my questions, hollered over the whine of the engines. It is more than basic aerodynamics that the pilot imparts to me; we are, after all, flying into the heart of the Bermuda Triangle. The Bahamas is one of only two places where the invisible magnetic lines that circle the globe are mysteriously broken, which is what caused old-fashioned compasses to spin erratically. And sure enough he shows me where the lines break on the flight map, at a spot southeast of New Providence Island. But we don't have to worry about that this morning, he assures me. Modern navigational instruments have overcome these irregularities in nature. Fear of the Bermuda Triangle is a thing of the past.

I envy his certitude. No doubt he grew up with easy access to all kinds of gadgets and machines. He betrays no ambivalence toward them; he trusts them implicitly. I marvel at the ease with which he manipulates the Cessna's controls. Technology has a way of eclipsing deeply rooted fears and replacing them . . . with what? I wish I knew. I feel like a moldy potato in a field full of succulent melons. I'm not so contemporary and up-to-date that I don't believe in unseen forces—hidden, lurking, inscrutable forces that can leap out at you like phantoms from a bog. If we pass over that spot southeast of New Providence Island, who's to say

88

the compass won't spin wildly, the props sputter and
fail, the aircraft plunge like a rock into the water?
That's the difference between the pilot and me; he be-
lieves in the efficacy of the technology he has mas-
tered. I don't know what I believe in—though as long
as I am sealed inside this fuselage, I will believe in the
efficacy of the machine and the man who flies it; as
soon as I arrive on the ground, I'll look around for
some other god.

At forty-six I'm probably fifteen years older than the
pilot. That's a significant difference in the postmodern
world, where new generations are calibrated according
to the longevity of TV shows and automotive trends.
My emotional make-up is decidedly anachronistic.
I look back to an earlier time; the clop of hooves on a
cobblestoned street tantalizes my imagination. For
some people the world is a smorgasbord of delights, to
be sampled eagerly and without hesitation. To others
it is still a smorgasbord, but the delights are laced with
microbes that can erupt into the bloodstream like dirty
little screws. Such is the cardinal difference, I warrant,
between a superstitious mentality and a scientific one.
Ah well, I always did fancy myself a transitional figure,
one foot planted firmly in the marsh of ancestral fear,
the other mincing cautiously across a parking lot toward an environmentally enclosed shopping mall.

In my own quixotic way, I keep looking for another
Saint-Exupéry, the Aviator Monk of my dreams. A person both contemplative and out-going, adventurous
and shy. Was Amelia Earhart one of the most interesting figures of the twentieth century, or am I barking
through a stovepipe hat? A figure of mythological pro-
portions, she disappeared over a remote Pacific island
while circling for a place to land. Who was she in reality? The historical record seems clear, though no
doubt there was some confusion in her own mind.

That 1937 around-the-world flight was to be her last, and who knows, from the vantage point of her later years, what conclusions she might have drawn from it? She was a thoughtful, sensitive woman with a gift for description and analysis. Amelia. Amelia. You are my favorite adventurer of this benighted century. Surely there were times when she felt like a fish in a glass bowl; anyone could look in, but she couldn't see out. The latest theory has her dying of dysentery in 1943 while a prisoner of the Japanese on Saipan. It is the fate of our gods and goddesses that we are forever altering the circumstances of their lives to fit our need for them to remain youthful and unchanged. The poor woman. Shitting herself to death, dehydrated as a prune, and no one lifting a finger to help. It is not a fate appropriate to a person of her accomplishments. The reality is too unforgiving. Even Icarus fell into the sea with a splash. I prefer to believe that Amelia, knowing that her time was up—like one of the Native American gods—went off into the wilderness and disappeared.

Andros, the biggest island in the Bahamas, passes underneath. A wide spongy mass, covered with scrub and palmettos, fringed with inlets and channels, dotted with pools and lagoons. The least known of the major islands, visited primarily by sportsmen and divers. Early settlers included Seminole Indians fleeing white encroachment in Florida. It is home of the chick-charnies, mischievous elves with three fingers, three toes, red eyes, scraggly beards, and green feathers; they hang upside down by their tails from the branches of silk cotton trees. Though largely benign, they are capable, when irritated, of twisting a man's head backwards on his shoulders.

I spot a few settlements on the fringe. The west coast is shallow, rising out of a creamy vanilla bank, splotched with coral heads and mangrove swamps.

A scrofulous-looking place. Excellent for bonefish, however. The east shore is rimmed by the third long-
est barrier reef in the world. From seven thousand feet
the reef is clearly visible, a spidery line of rubble skirting the coast. Beyond it, inky as the discharge from a
squid, lurks the abysmal depths of the Tongue of the
Ocean. British and American submarines cavort in secret war games here. This morning the indigo surface
is hammered into a marbled pattern of white-crested
waves.

In the morning light, disconcertingly brilliant despite the scrim of clouds, Andros spills across a varie-
gated sea. Life is ephemeral out here, the landforms as
elusive as shadows. Everything is so calm, so tranquil,
so beguiling . . . so deceptively lethal. Death mas-
querades in innocent garb. A flowering tree, a curling
wave, a splashing fish, a man on a motorscooter wearing a yellow cap with a red bobble. Wherever you go,
from Bimini down to Grand Turk, Death follows you
like a porter waiting for the opportunity to take the
suitcase out of your hand and deposit it in a room
along with thousands of other pieces of unclaimed luggage. It's just a feeling I get; it has as much to do with
the dazzling immensity of space as it does with any
phobia or fear. No matter where I look, the sky seems
to blur with the sea as if someone had wet their finger
and run it along the edge of a watercolor.

Shadows cast by clouds upon the sea give the illusion
of islands. Ineffable landforms, chimerical ideograms
that dissolve and regroup as the day progresses. The
tallest point in the Bahamas reaches 206 feet on a
gnarly ridge overlooking Cat Island. A mild glacier
melt today could spell disaster for the archipelago,
which was once a connected mass of oolitic limestone.
Life clings precariously to every available perch. With
their modest profiles, the islands are difficult to detect
at sea; from the air they resemble jagged flagstones

mossed with verdant fur. Their impermanence marks a
critical difference between islands and continents. You
need more than your imagination to hold onto out
here. You need family and friends, hot music and
good rum, a shady spot to play cards, a few chickens
and a garden, a boat with an engine that won't conk
out. You need an ego as flexible as a kite, tethered to a
fixed point with a stout cord. Sooner or later everything, including the souls of the dead that haunt the
graveyards, swirls up into the air.

The chatter of the Cessna's engines is sweetly com-
forting. Sitting in the copilot's seat, I pantomime my
favorite role, acolyte to a priest in charge of a special
mission. (Every day at boarding school I donned a
black gown and white surplice and aided the rector in
the service; my chief job was dropping the hymnal
numbers into the proper slots so the congregation
would know what to sing.) The performance this time
is catalytic. Through the miracle of the flying machine, I am propelled without fanfare into the heart of
mystery. Nowhere do I feel my life so rectified as in an
airplane cockpit. Everything has its proper function:
switches, dials, throttles, flaps . . . while I myself
monitor the incessant transformation of thought and
image by remaining as stationary as a hunter trying to
conjure up the figure of a wild turkey or deer.

Behind me, down the length of the narrow fuselage,
voices yap and murmur, but there is little joking and
almost no laughter. Flying doesn't foster the same camaraderie as a lengthy sea voyage. Under the con-
straints of speed and the anxiety it creates, the mind
turns inward to a kind of stony pasture tufted with dry
grass. One woman keeps her eyes riveted upon the
pages of a glossy historical novel. The others betray
an edgy impatience, like people in a hospital waiting
room. We are all anxious to get to Georgetown.

"Staniel Cay," the pilot mutters, pointing a finger at a narrow island drifting upon the sea like a discolored stick. Through binoculars, I make out a slim runway bisecting the southern tip. Beveled around the rim with tawny sand, Staniel is one of a series of cays that lead down to Great Exuma. Many of the cays are uninhabited; they serve as private lairs for fishermen, pleasure boaters, and drug runners.

At the axis of the cays we alter our course south-southeast, dip under a patch of scruffy clouds, and follow the cays down toward Great Exuma. The pilot announces that we are twenty minutes from Georgetown. The passengers begin to stir. We are nearing our destination. The warm air rising off the cays causes the aircraft to bounce and sway. The sun glances off the metal wings with a blinding glare. Dark channels indicating navigable depths separate the islands. The surface of the water is checkered with contrasting blue and green patches. Cloud shadows splotch the sea out toward the horizon, creating the illusion of an infinitesimal profusion of cays. In the distance, Great Exuma rises out of the water like the shell of a Hawksbill turtle.

Georgetown, capital of the Exumas, lies in the heart of the Bahamas, right at the latitude of the Tropic of Cancer. Theoretically, at noon on the day of the summer solstice, a person standing on the line would cast no shadow. The sun would beam directly overhead; his shadow would be tightly contained within the cylinder of his body. He would project no silhouette or immaterial extension of any part of his body; everything would be directly absorbed by the sun. He would have no past or future, no history or destiny, no memory or hope of fulfillment. He would be totally enveloped in a cone of light.

I write this nonsense in my head every day. Travel

brings out the best and worst, the limitations and excesses; it does not cultivate a reasonable middle ground. Everything observed and felt clamors to be translated into myth. The echo of an inner voice yearning for recognition generates a volatile chemistry between the heart and brain. Odyssean impulses. Sinbadian reveries. Certain locations on the map, as if by magnetic fix, cause the imagination to confabulate in unexpected ways. The urge to travel is synonymous with the compulsion to recreate the world in more meaningful terms. We are all Marco Polos of the spirit, seeking our vision of the spires of distant Cathay.

As the plane angles down toward the coppiced bulge of Great Exuma, it encounters a layer of warm air. The wings vibrate with a vigor that makes the passengers shift uneasily. As the Cessna passes over the northwest rim of the island, the altimeter dips below two thousand feet. Mangrove swamps form a marshy barrier along the shallow banks of the leeward coast. The interior of the island is forested with a thick growth of palmetto and scrub. Brush fires spiral into the air. Off the left wing I see the tin-roofed houses of Georgetown; beyond them, the snake-like profile of Stocking Island. The field is dead ahead, a strip of yellow limestone broiling in the midday sun. The pilot lowers the wheels and extends the flaps. The Cessna's speed diminishes. The passengers square around in their seats. All talking ceases. The pilot throttles back, corrects the drift, throttles back some more. Aiming, guiding, guying the craft on course. We are speeding toward a fateful rendezvous. We are threading the eye of a momentous needle, and while we are unlikely to emerge transformed on the other side, we will finally be disburdened of a nagging uneasiness.

The narrow strip, pocked and lumpy, strewn with wrecked aircraft, rises up to kiss our wheels. Land. We are landing. The contact throws us forward against our belts. The wheels skip into the air then touch down again. Behind me somebody gasps. Another whistles. A third breaks into song. The pilot reverses the props and applies the brakes. The headlong forward glide we initiated in Miami winds down to a sluggish crawl. The plane and its cargo settle into the comfortable embrace of gravity. We are down. Inside the fuselage there is cheering and clapping. The pilot grins and waves his hand. The aircraft rolls along the bumpy apron then makes a wide turn and trundles back toward the terminal. A black man in a tight blue shirt stands squarely on a faded yellow mark clutching a pair of wooden blocks. The airplane stutters toward him. The pilot brings the nose up to within a few feet of his impassive face and switches off the engines. The propellers wheeze to a halt. We are down. The rear hatch swings open. A whiff of humid air permeates the cabin. I congratulate the pilot on a job well done. "Routine," he replies with a diffident smile. "Routine. Routine."

Point Center

CAIRO, ILLINOIS

I came by car, crossing the Mississippi River at Cape Girardeau and descending the narrow two-lane highway that skirts the wooded bluffs on the Illinois shore. I drove past the drowsy village of Thebes, where Abraham Lincoln once delivered a campaign oration. South of Thebes the bluffs sputtered out into a broad, fertile bottomland. The time was mid-November, and the trees were shorn of leaves; a feeble sun glimmered between gray strips of stationary clouds. Tenant shacks crowded the road; a few were occupied, but most stood empty and rotting. The shacks were raised on blocks above the ground. In this flat country near the confluence of two great rivers, floodwater was an annual fact of life. Cotton had once been grown in the alluvial deposits. Now only a few small fields were under cultivation. In the brittle November light the landscape looked as if it had been sucked dry by a pump and then abandoned for the crows and blackbirds to pick over.

North of Cairo the exit ramp of the Chicago to Memphis interstate disgorged few automobiles at midday. The two-lane road curved into town past more shacks, then a sprinkling of weathered brick buildings, and finally an assortment of dilapidated stores and run-down residences. The town had an empty, vacant look. A handful of people plodded listlessly through the streets. By the time I reached the other side near the juncture of the rivers, a disquieting sensation nibbled at my stomach. Something was gravely wrong here. This was not what I had come to see.

At the tip of the tongue of land near the confluence was a modest park with a concrete observation tower. A path of cracked and broken rocks bumped down a slope to the tip. I picked my way past rings of burned-out fires and piles of empty bottles and cans. So here I was at last. Point Center. At the nexus of the North American continent. To my left yawned the mouth of the Ohio. To my right, low from the summer drought, chugged the sluggish Mississippi.

If the North American continent can be described as having a navel, Cairo is it. The rivers that converge here form an umbilicus that binds mountains to prairies, north woods to marshy deltas. At the center of this flux lies Cairo—*locus classicus,* the hub around which all these forces congregate and disperse.

I had thought about Cairo for a long time. Hanging on the wall of my New York apartment in the 1960s was a reproduction of a nineteenth-century map of the Ohio and Mississippi river valleys. The map held a puzzling fascination for me. Sober, I would make note of the towns and villages that lined the banks of the rivers, and try to imagine what they must have looked like. Drunk, I would trace a circle with my finger from *Point* southeast Missouri through southern Illinois, down *Center:* into western Kentucky and Tennessee, over to Arkan- *Cairo,* sas and back up to Missouri—a shaky, unsteady circle *Illinois* that had at its center the modest dot of Cairo, Illinois.

Two bridges near the confluence spanned the rivers, one crossing into Missouri, the other into Kentucky. I ignored both and got back into the car and drove into Cairo to take a closer look. What I saw was not at all promising. Huge holes pocked the side streets branching off toward the levee wall bordering the Ohio River. Weeds flourished in vacant lots. Empty store-fronts gaped like hollow sockets. A woman in a wool cap and quilted parka combed through the contents of a dumpster. Idlers hung out on corners, yakking and gesturing, drinking from containers wrapped in plain brown bags.

I parked near the levee wall and got out. A tugboat was nudging a string of empty barges up the Ohio River toward the Kentucky bridge. On a nearby cor-ner'stood the two-story Cairo National Bank. Delicate lintels arched across the tops of the windows; wedge-like quoins anchored the front corners from the side-walk to the roof. An incised date over the front en-trance read 1906. It had been an attractive building, but no more: the roof was missing, the windows were broken out, the second floor had collapsed into a pile of charred beams and rubble.

From an elderly fellow standing in front of the levee watching the barges, I learned that the bank had burned in 1985 and never been repaired.

"Oh, this was once a *bursting* town," the old man reminisced in a wistful voice. "There were twenty thousand people here, and anybody who wanted to could get work. The freight cars from Chicago came through by the hundreds, and the river was jammed with barges lined up to unload right where we're standing."

He twitched his thin shoulders and pulled the zipper on his jacket up to his throat. He pronounced the name of the town as "CARE-oh," with a gliding emphasis on the first syllable.

"It's all gone to seed now," he sighed. "The kids skedaddle out of here for St. Louis or Memphis the instant they graduate from high school. There's nothing left but us old folks and these empty streets and this bunch of broken-down buildings."

He gazed over at the trees lining the Kentucky shore. "It's sad to see your hometown come to this after all these years," he muttered in a voice somewhere between a whisper and a growl.

At one time Cairo's location boded well for the establishment of a major metropolis. A Jesuit priest, Pierre Francis Xavier de Charlevoix, reported in 1721 that the land between the rivers was of immense strategic importance. In 1818, the Illinois Territorial Legislature drew up plans for a city. Lured by growing river traffic, squatters and woodcutters settled on the land. They were a verminous lot, given to drink, thievery, and whoring. The location was unimpressive. No high bluffs commanded a view of the countryside. The town sprawled across a swampy appendage between two unruly rivers that annually overflowed their banks. The sodden ground was a virulent habitat for mosquitoes; diseases like malaria and yellow fever were a chronic problem.

Serious development did not begin until the 1830s. The Cairo City and Canal Company formulated elaborate plans for levees, canals, factories, and warehouses. But the levees failed to hold back the rampaging water,

and the company's insistence upon leasing lots, rather
than selling them, turned away prospective customers.
For years the town remained little more than a motley
collection of shacks and huts. Charles Dickens, who
chugged past the site on his first North American tour
in 1842, called it "a dismal swamp, on which the half-
built houses rot away . . . a hotbed of disease, an ugly
sepulchre, a grave uncheered by any gleam of promise: a place without one single quality, in earth or air
or water, to commend it: such is this dismal Cairo."

Granted Dickens had an ax to grind. Reportedly, he
was a victim of a land bubble scheme perpetuated by
the Cairo City and Canal Company that sold fraudu-
lent bonds through a London banking firm to gullible
investors. Dickens later satirized the scam and its victims in his novel *Martin Chuzzlewit* (1843). His feelings
for practically everything he observed in North America during that trip were similarly negative.

The 1850s brought many changes to Cairo. Lots
were made available at reasonable prices. In 1854 the
Illinois Central extended its tracks down from Chicago. And then came the Civil War, which dramatically altered the town's fortunes. The important location was recognized by both sides. On April 22—ten
days after the South Carolina militia fired on Fort
Sumter—Union soldiers occupied the town.

Throughout the war, Cairo proved to be a vital supply depot for the Union Army. A critical component
of federal strategy was to seize control of the Mississippi from St. Louis to the Gulf, thus dividing the
Confederacy. Cairo, at the tip of Illinois—wedged
like a splinter between the slave states of Kentucky and
Missouri—was a natural springboard for the invasion.
Overnight the town swelled like a tick on the sweet
blood of war. Men and material poured into the region,
accompanied by the campfollowers and spongers who
feed off such a lavish host. The banks of both rivers

were packed with barges, sternwheelers, and gunships; the dusty streets were thronged with military and civilian hustlers.

A future hero of the conflict, Ulysses S. Grant, launched his first campaign from Cairo in the fall of 1861. It was from Cairo that he led a successful assault the following winter on Fort Donelson in Tennessee. One can imagine Grant in October 1861, then an unseasoned brigadier, climbing a levee, peering across the Ohio River into the dark forests of Kentucky, and brooding about what sort of destiny lay in store for him. Transformed by the exigencies of national disaster into a brawling entrepot of patriotic fervor, Cairo played a significant role in the subjugation of the Confederacy; and then, in the aftermath, under pressure of westward expansion, it began to wither and decline. The soldiers marched away, the whores disappeared, the blacksmiths and sutlers packed up, and Cairo began to fade like an old print exposed to the sun. Railway lines marching boldly across the Midwest offered more efficient shortcuts between the burgeoning industrial cities than what the rivers could provide.

I ate a delicious lunch of red beans and rice in a restaurant on the main drag. Midway through the meal, an ambulance screamed past the window. One or two heads rose above their plates with a kind of torpid curiosity; the slow babble filling the air quickened for a few seconds before resuming its normal pace.

One wall of the establishment was covered with aerial photographs. A glossy picture taken in 1975 showed downtown Cairo completely swamped by floodwaters. "That must have been a real mess," I remarked to the waitress.

"Oh, it wasn't so bad," she replied, filling up my glass with sugary tea. "The water only got to about three foot in the street out there."

"What did you do?"

"Why, we just put on hip boots and went on serving food. Nothin' much else we could do. We didn't get no relief from anybody for nearly a week."

"I bet that was irritating."

"Not really. We're used to being stranded in this town."

After lunch I drove at a leisurely pace through the residential district north of downtown. A bumpy brick-cobbled street angled diagonally away from the main drag and the sound of belching trucks and buzzing motorcycles. It was quiet back there, pleasant. The green grass of the better-kept lawns was covered with crinkly orange leaves. School must have let out closeby; groups of children ambled along the sidewalks. What a contrast between this neighborhood and the blight downtown! Located only a few blocks apart, they were like sections of two different worlds haphazardly plunked down next to one another.

An imposing mansion stood on the corner of a narrow lot shaded by tall magnolia trees. The house must have been built by a kingfish of substance, for it dwarfed all the others in the neighborhood. The house had three stories and was constructed like a fortress out of red bricks and mortar. Wrought iron balconies edged the front steps and porch; narrow windows soared up the brick sides like gun portals. A square tower notched with additional windows projected over the roof like a turret.

"Who lives in this house now?" I asked a group of passing kids.

"Old Lady Blade," a girl responded. "And she's so mean she can bite your head off!"

103

"She'll let you go through the house if you want," said another girl. "There are people in there who'll show you the furniture and drapes. I bet they'll even show you the old lady. She's real old. She don't get out of bed much anymore."

They gamboled on down the street, scattering leaves with their quick feet. I sat down on the high curb in front of Old Lady Blade's house and lit a cigarette. Houses like hers in funky old river towns represent the acme of cultural achievement. Aesthetically they are usually the most interesting structures. Why was there such a profound gap between the fruits of private enterprise and the attitude toward public buildings? The contrast between this neighborhood and the mess downtown was almost criminal. Did the term private enterprise imply lack of public consciousness? Did people make money primarily to construct private cloisters behind which they could retreat like monks?

I had seen all I needed of my mythical metropolis of the interior. The reality was grueling and unpleasant; Cairo had reached its apogee long ago and now was orbiting swiftly away from the sun. Nothing could redeem this town, not the belated largesse of Old Lady Blade, not even massive quantities of federal money. Maybe the rivers in the next flood should reclaim the spongy turf on which the city moldered. Maybe the waitress in the restaurant and all the other tough birds downtown who keep hanging gamely on should just climb into a boat and paddle off to someplace else. Biology tells us plainly what to expect when individual cells begin to die off faster than they can be replaced. But for an entire community to sicken and falter—especially a community with the historical resonances of Cairo—defies analysis. It is more than an act of the gods, and yet something considerably less. It is the juggernaut of history delivered with a resounding crunch. It is the brutal, implacable fact of small-town American life in the late twentieth century.

Along the main drag leading out of town toward the bridges a considerable crowd had gathered. The time was late afternoon; the sky was streaked with moody gray clouds. Next to the brick wall of a grocery store a fire truck had pulled up and was parked facing the wrong direction; the pink light crowning the yellow-green cab flashed soundlessly. A handful of sheriff's deputies were waving traffic through a narrow lane on the congested street. "We need the road cleared," a deputy barked at me. "We got a medivac helicopter coming in from Cape Girardeau. There's been an accident."

I parked the car on a side street and joined the crowd in front of the grocery store. The paramedic ambulance that had screamed by the restaurant an hour earlier was present, its lights flashing and its doors flung open. The crowd was tight-lipped and grim. People massed along the curb or spilled out into the street. They stood in loose, uneasy groups or by themselves, whispering and muttering. Periodically an outraged voice fluttered up from the dull murmur of shock and dismay that muffled the scene like a blanket.

Two boys pedaling home from a nearby school on a single bicycle had been clobbered by an oil truck. One of the boys was sitting up in the street a few feet from the curb being comforted by his mother. She had her arms wrapped around his shoulders, and she was murmuring something into his ear. The boy's pale cheeks were starchy with dried tears. He clung numbly to his mother and opened and shut his mouth like a marionette animated by a slack string. A soft, retching sound bubbled between his swollen lips.

105

Nearby were the mangled remains of the bicycle and the body of the other boy. He lay on his back against the gritty asphalt like a clump of straw, his arms splayed out limply at his sides. His bare feet were rubbery and lifeless, and they were slowly turning blue. A doctor was attending to him, along with several firemen. The doctor had performed a tracheotomy to unclog his windpipe. IV tubes had been inserted into his ankles and wrists. Two firemen clutching plasma bags stood over the boy. A third held the black nozzle of an oxygen mask against his nose and mouth. Earlier when the doctor had commenced CPR on his heart, the boy had vomited up a mass of sticky blood. Twice the boy's heart had stopped and twice the doctor, working feverishly, had started it again.

At the back of the crowd a corpulent man in a three-piece suit clung with both arms to the waist of an ashen-faced woman. "My son!" she screamed. "He's my son! I have a right to be with my son!" She pulled and strained against the man's strong arms, but he wouldn't let go. A sheriff's deputy extended one long arm and touched her lightly on the shoulder as if doing what he could to restrain her. The woman's features were bunched into a puffy red knot at the center of her grieving face. Her voice whipped over the crowd with an electric crackle.

The driver of the oil truck sat in the sheriff's car in the middle of the street staring blankly through the front window. No one spoke to him. No one even approached him. He sat totally alone like a man who has never had a bright word said about him in his lifetime.

The medivac helicopter from Cape Girardeau finally hovered into view over an hour after the accident had occurred. Deputies cleared the street of automobiles and pedestrians; with considerable skill the pilot threaded the chopper through a narrow slot between telephone wires and power lines. A paramedic

leaped out the rear hatch carrying an orange case, followed by an orderly toting a stretcher. The paramedic
glided across the street on urgent strides. He dropped
down next to the boy and consulted with the doctor.
On their knees, their heads nearly touching, they
made an odd pair, like gardeners discussing the roots
of an exotic plant or sandlot athletes diagramming a
complicated play. The dull gray light, the restrained
silence of the onlookers, the whirling bulbs of the
emergency vehicles contributed to the eerie sense of
unreality.

Stretching out one hand with the forefinger extended as if in slow motion, the paramedic indicated
the spot where the orderly should place the stretcher.
Then, after additional consultation with the doctor
and firemen, the team closed in on the boy, and, slipping their hands gingerly under the inert body, they
elevated it off the pavement and shifted it onto the
stretcher. From the back of the crowd the mother continued to cry out and plead. "I have a right to see him!"
she wailed. "I have a right! He's my son! He's my son!"
And then gently, as if it were the fragilest of objects,
the team hoisted the stretcher into the air, and bobbing
together in an ungainly cluster, clutching bags and
tubes and IV needles, heads down, eyes slotted against
the wash of throdding rotors, they advanced toward
the helicopter. The orderly secured the stretcher inside the fuselage; one by one the doctor and the firemen relinquished their paraphernalia to the orderly
and the paramedic and backed away across the street.
The last thing I saw before the hatch was closed
was the paramedic pressing down on the boy's chest
with the heel of his left hand. Pressing and pressing
with a steady, metronomic beat, like a farmer trying to
coax water up the stem of a rusty pump.

With a ratchety swirl the helicopter rose into the
air, missing the wires by a few feet before twirling over

the rooftops and speeding out of sight. The ascent of the craft seemed to pull something with it, a measure of awe and silence, leaving in its wake a residue of bitterness and despair. The people of Cairo stood around the bleak street grumbling among themselves. A bearded man in shapeless fatigues and a ratty, camouflaged jacket balled and unballed the fingers of both hands into angry fists. Another lectured a small group, blaming the no-account mayor for the tragedy. A group of women consoled one another by raising their voices in protest against the dilatory politicians who had failed to provide adequate services for the people. Meanwhile, at the back of the dissolving crowd, the man in the three-piece suit continued to clutch the distraught mother around the waist. His face was pale and drawn; his cheeks and forehead looked as if they had been dusted with a chalkboard eraser. Someone mentioned driving the woman to the hospital at Cape Girardeau. Another ran off to find a car. The woman was so racked with violent sobbing she could barely stand. Three or four people literally pressed themselves against her from all sides, as if trying, with the weight and solidity of their bodies, to keep her anguish from spilling into the street like a cracked egg.

I wandered between groups of grumbling people. "How come it took so long for help to get here?" I asked an elderly woman.

"'Cause there's no ambulance in this town. 'Cause there's no hospital or clinic. 'Cause there's no nothing."

Her voice was gravelly with suppressed rage. The smooth cheeks of her black face glowed dully in the afternoon light like a polished stone.

"Where did the ambulance come from?" I said.

"Mound City. And that's a few miles away from here."

"Where do you go if you get sick, then?"

"The nearest hospital's at the Cape or over in Paducah."

108

"But what do you do if you have an emergency like a heart attack?"

"You die, that's what you do. You die like a dog in the streets like that white boy just did."

She glared at me with ill-disguised contempt. "You don't live here, do you?"

"No, ma'am, I don't."

"Figures," she said, and shuffled off.

I slipped across the wide street where traffic was starting to flow again at a normal pace. It was late afternoon, and the oncoming night was starting to crowd the last streaks of light into a narrow band along the western horizon. A heavy weight, solid and insupportable, had settled in my stomach. An image from my boyhood congealed on the surface of my memory. I used to delight in filling a metal bucket with water from the garden hose and swinging it around by the handle in a tight circle to see if any water would spill out. It never ceased to amaze me how the force of my revolving arm thrust the water against the sides, opening a hole in the center that seemed to funnel down to an uncertain depth. For me it posed a problem that I never really understood. How was it that certain forces, nominally energetic and promising, were able to create a void in the center of the physical body they inhabited?

The rumble of distant thunder sounded faintly through the air. In the east the sky had grown ugly and menacing. I reached the car and took out my keys. Before opening the door, I looked back across the street. The final remnants of the crowd had dispersed. Shoppers were emerging from the grocery store with armloads of brown sacks. From a side panel in the yellow-green truck a fireman uncoiled a long canvas hose. Clasping the nozzle with both hands, he washed the last stains of the boy's blood into the gutter.

Point Center: Cairo, Illinois

A Black Hills
Encounter

Hurra for the prairies and the swift
antelope. They fleet by the hunter
like flashes or meteors.

John James Audubon

I was tramping up and down the hills, watching carefully for buffalo. It was late spring, too early for the
rutting season, though a few calves had recently been
born, and it wasn't a good idea to get too near the
cows. A hiker who steps between a calf and its mother
runs the risk of being trampled. The bulls were grazing
by themselves, solitary dots far out on the slopes of
the hills. As I walked I kept close to the trees. Buffalo
are unpredictable, and if one charges, the safest place
to be is up in a tree. As high up as you can get, with,
preferably, a comfortable branch to sit on. The buffalo
might not leave for a while; he might even decide to
spend the rest of the day cropping grass at the foot of
the tree. A man I know who was once caught out in
the open by a small band of buffalo wisely sat down

111

Sundancers and made himself as inconspicuous as possible. He
and crossed his legs yoga-style, bowed his head, and be-
River gan to pray. Buffalo stirred all around; one or two even
Demons nudged him in the back with their wet noses, but he
wasn't harmed. He remained in that position for three
hours until the band disappeared over a hill.

The afternoon was gloomy. Dark clouds muscled
down over the lower slopes of the Black Hills. I was
trying to locate the creek where the summer before I
had stumbled upon a rack of bleached buffalo bones.
The sun had been hot that day, the grass parched and
dry. It was the rutting season, and when the wind was
right I could hear bulls roaring all over the park. I
came across several wallows—patches of bare earth
sticky with piss and excrement where buffalo roll to rid
themselves of flies. The stench from these mires was
blinding. Squatting beside one, I felt as if I were looking into a hole that disappeared deep into the earth to
a place that no longer existed, not even in the mind of
the oldest living human. A tunnel that drilled deep
through human memory to a time when such sights
out here on the Great Plains had been commonplace.

But the time now was early June, the grass shagging
the hills of Wind Cave National Park was bright green,
and the buffalo were scattered far back into the trees.
Down in the woody draws, vines and bushes grew in
thick profusion. Birds flitted incessantly, fashioning
nests. The long harsh winter had ended, and everything was in motion, eager to foliate according to genetic prescription. Summer in South Dakota is short
and leaves little margin for dawdling. Birds and animals know this and go about their business with an
urgency far different from their southern counterparts.

I crossed the road that skirts the eastern rim of the
park and stepped carefully through a prairie-dog village. My presence was greeted with a flurry of squeaks

and chirps, each watchdog at the hole passing on the signal to the next before disappearing. These animals are voracious eaters, and the terrain was shorn of grass. Ranchers detest them, and more than one politician in South Dakota has been elected to office on an anti–prairie dog platform. Their natural predators include badgers, coyotes, hawks, and black-footed ferrets. Extensive poisoning of prairie dogs has resulted, curiously, in the virtual elimination of the black-footed ferret. This is unfortunate, as a few ferrets are capable of controlling the population of a prairie-dog village. The prairie dogs cohabit with the ferrets, even occupy the same holes. Many ranchers, however, don't want prairie dogs anywhere on their land. They regard them as the worst sort of pest, whose sole purpose is to devour the forage that properly belongs to their cattle. A few ranchers have proposed a radical solution—the elimination of the prairie dog. Thus is illustrated one of the cardinal differences between animals and men; while ferrets can reduce the numbers of prairie dogs to acceptable levels, only man can exterminate them all.

I started up the hill away from the prairie dogs. The nearest tree was several hundred yards away. I walked softly, my boots crunching the new grass. My plan was to ease up to the crown of the hill and peer over the rim. My concern was that just over the rim a buffalo might be grazing. And then I'd have to make a decision. And then, with my heart clacking in my throat, I'd have to ease back down the hill, diagonally toward the trees on my left. Or beat a hasty retreat straight through the prairie dog village to the road. Or, after praying fervently, be transported to the other side of the hill by a providential windspout.

(Provided I saw the buffalo first and it chose to ignore me, the first two contingencies were possible. Should the beast take offense at my presence, the third was my only hope. Few men—and certainly none my age—have ever outrun a buffalo.)

Just then a head appeared over the rim. I gulped and clutched my walking stick. Silhouetted against the gray sky, its features obscured in shadow, the animal displayed a narrow skull and a set of distinctive horns. It wasn't a buffalo, thank fortune, but an antelope. With a graceful, stately gait it ambled over the top of the hill. The black horns poking out from the sleek skull were pronged at the tips like darning needles. The animal moved with a casual grace that belied its extraordinary power. The underbelly, lower legs, and throat were white; the back and tubular body a creamy buff color. After the horns the legs were the most remarkable feature; they were long and shapely and feminine, with muscular thighs joined high up on a solid body. The legs tapered delicately to dark hooves; compared with the meaty thighs the ankles were disproportionately slim. The fastest animal on the North American continent, the antelope is capable of speeds over forty miles per hour. A large chest cavity and oversized heart circulates blood rapidly. Adorning the handsome rump was a cowl of white hair. When alarmed, the hair flashes and expands, signaling other antelope of danger.

The animal sauntered down the hill. Twenty feet away it stopped, looked around, then looked straight at me. The expression in its liquid eyes sent a thrill through my body all the way to my toes. It looked at me plainly, without artifice or design, with forthright curiosity. A breeze whirled over the hill and flowed past us, rippling my shirt. The prairie dogs I had passed earlier didn't regard me this way, and neither had the buffalo. Their gaze was sullen and suspicious, whereas the prairie dogs had jumped all over me with their panicky eyes. The antelope's gaze was different:

114

measured, temperate, steady, assured. The gaze of a A Black Hills Encounter
self-contained woman: cool, elusive, irresistible.

Reaching out, first with one dainty forehoof then
the other, the antelope scraped at the grass. Then,
squatting gingerly, it relieved itself.

What was going on here? Was this some kind of
salutation? Perhaps my own scent had triggered the
creature's bladder. Or perhaps this was the way the
pronghorn signaled its acceptance of me, its nonfear.

A century ago the pronghorn would have bolted at my
scent. In the early 1800s there were thirty to forty million pronghorn antelope in North America. Today
there are four hundred thousand. We have become so
inured to the spectacle of mass death that we cannot
begin to fathom the indescribable slaughter of animals
that took place on this continent during the nineteenth
century. Buffalo, as many as sixty million. Pronghorn
antelope, more than thirty million. Grizzly bears, several hundred thousand. Passenger pigeons, a few bil-
lion. The list of eradicated species forms a melancholy
roll: Great Auk, Carolina Parakeet, Sea Mink, Steller's
Sea Cow, Labrador Duck, Audubon Big Horn Sheep,
Passenger Pigeon, Heath Hen, Ivory-Billed Woodpecker. Nothing less than an all-out assault against
wildlife. An attempt, in the name of progress and expansion, to transform the American wilderness into an
orderly and fruitful garden, a "peaceable kingdom" of
domesticity and animal husbandry.

A baleful precedent was established during the
1800s, which can be linked to the ghastly slaughter of
human beings in the twentieth century. That may
sound farfetched, but if human beings can extirpate an
entire species of animal, what's to prevent them from

killing an entire race of people? The Nazis tried it during World War II and nearly succeeded; more recently, in Cambodia, the Khymer Rouge massacred a quarter of its population in the name of a half-baked Marxist ideology.

What happens to people when they realize that they can eradicate an entire species with impunity? The quantification of death becomes an all-absorbing spectacle; a desperate numbers game develops. Devising an efficient system to kill other creatures becomes a kind of intellectual problem that requires not only considerable organization but the collusion of the entire population, not just those who pull the triggers.

Trapping or netting passenger pigeons was an effective way to kill them, but even more effective was to thrust up the barrel of the old cannon on the village green and fire a load of scrap iron and nails into a dense flock passing overhead. Two or three blasts, and the sky literally rained dead pigeons. A system for killing great auks took advantage of their herd mentality. Landing on lonely North Atlantic islands where the birds nested every spring, hunters propped up long planks between the shore and their rowboats. Once they got the flightless birds to follow one another up the planks, one man armed with a club could bash in thousands of skulls. Buffalo hunting, once considered a dangerous pursuit on horseback when the hunter was armed with a bow and arrow, became by the 1870s little more than an exercise in target practice for men equipped with long-range rifles.

These deeds were not committed exclusively by illiterate hunters and bloodthirsty freebooters. We have only to read Francis Parkman's autobiography, *The Oregon Trail*, to realize that the antipathy toward animal life was fundamental to nineteenth-century thought. "An old buffalo bull is a brute of unparalleled ugliness,"

116

he declares. "At first sight of him every feeling of pity vanishes." Upon encountering a white wolf on the plains, Parkman observes, "He was an ugly scoundrel, with a bushy tail, a large head, and a most repulsive countenance." Later, noting the behavior of another buffalo, he offers this account:

Sometimes an old bull would step forward, and gaze at me with a grim and stupid countenance; then he would turn and butt his next neighbor; then he would lie down and roll over in the dust, kicking his hoofs in the air. When satisfied with this amusement, he would jerk his head and shoulders upward, and resting on his forelegs, stare at me in this position, half blinded by his mane, and his face covered with dirt; then up he would spring upon all fours, shake his dusty sides, turn half around, and stand with his beard touching the ground, in an attitude of profound abstraction, as if reflecting on his puerile conduct. "You are too ugly to live," thought I; and aiming at the ugliest, I shot three of them in succession.

Parkman's puritanical New England sensibility would not tolerate the presence of evil inside himself. Instead, that evil was always *out there*, lurking like an imp in the trees, ready to pounce upon the innocent adventurer. It is only in the waning years of the twentieth century, after decades of furious bloodletting, that a profound shift has occurred in the human sensibility. And while it is not our place to gloat over the appearance of that shift, it is our responsibility to make sure that the consequences are properly acknowledged and maintained. Where people once found it convenient and even natural to locate the enemy in the body of an alien creature such as a wolf or a buffalo, today it is necessary that we recognize the presence inside ourselves and learn to live correctly with this terrible and frightening knowledge.

117

If one has become conditioned to think apocalyptically, how great a leap is it then from wiping out a species of animal to killing every member of a certain human kind? Once humanity becomes conditioned to expunging individual species, it becomes easier to rationalize the liquidation of creatures located elsewhere along the evolutionary chain. Especially when, in the case of the buffalo and the passenger pigeon, there seems to be so many of them. Genocide is the most monstrous crime that can be perpetrated against the earth. There is no barbarity more incomprehensible, more antithetical to the spirit of life, than the deliberate destruction of an entire kind of creature or plant.

What sort of people would execute this type of crime? What sort of people would kill a creature, not to eat it or salvage its pelt, but simply *to watch it die?* Such activity is the ultimate blasphemy, an implacable refutation of the natural will to live and multiply, a crime that not even Satan at his most vicious or turgid could have devised.

The pronghorn circled downwind and crept closer. I wasn't afraid. I was wary, and I wondered if it ever attacked humans, but I wasn't afraid. I was curious to touch it, to smell it, to experience it up close with my skin. Evidently the animal knew that the stick in my hand wasn't a weapon. Early travelers reported that antelope meat was sweet to eat. I wouldn't have the pleasure, though I might have something else: an encounter, a confrontation. In the animal's elegant form there was something decidedly sexual. I longed to run my hand along its rump and flanks.

California Indians, encountering grizzly bears on lonely mountain paths, sometimes ran headlong into them, hoping to pass through, transformed, to the other side. Suddenly I felt a physical urge to merge with this antelope, to *become* it . . . to sprout horns, to see long distances, to run forty miles per hour . . . to evolve into something both animal and human, a hybrid creature.

But no, it was impossible. My distinctness was complete, the distance between us inviolable. In order to become the animal I would have to kill it and eat it and wear its skin around my body and retain some piece—a bone or feature—as a talisman. And I was at least a hundred years too late for that. I could only look at it, approach cautiously, exchange stares; it was not my fate to smell its blood or taste its flesh. Like so many activities of the twentieth century, I was reduced to the role of a spectator, a watcher with intent, curious eyes. And while I was delighted that it was protected by law and couldn't be indiscriminately slaughtered, I regretted that I could not stalk it as part of a complex ritual. What is the difference then? When does ritual slaying degenerate into wanton killing? When the animal is regarded as an integer rather than a coeval mystery. When the communion between the two is no longer propitiatory, and the sound of a gun barking in the hunter's hands becomes the coveted sensation.

At last, its curiosity sated, the antelope stepped on down the hill. Raindrops peppered my bare scalp. Behind me, on the flat stretch of ground, the prairie dogs were squeaking with alarm. Something had moved into their camp, perhaps a hungry badger. I was hungry too. Clutching my stick, I walked down the hill, whistling softly, whistling in time to the crunch of my boots against the grass.

Cities
on the Plain

The year was 1955. I was fifteen years old. Short,
slight, nearsighted, with hornrims, butched hair
brushed up into a feeble imitation of a flattop, a rash of
pimples clustered around the corners of a yearning
mouth. My interests were diverse: football, modern
jazz, and colorful birds. I was an avid reader of Erskine
Caldwell novels, and when he spoke of Darlin' Jill's
"rising beauties" a warm flush spread through my loins.
I was aware that a galaxy of new suns was dawning inside me, and, try as I might to distract my attention,
those suns were heating up every part of my body.

My older brother had fallen into a snowbank on a
mountainside near Boulder, Colorado, while attending
summer school at the university. He had passed out
from drinking too much gin and beer and had con-

tracted acute pneumonia. His lungs had filled with fluid, and he lay in a hospital room in Denver with tubes running out his nose and mouth. Though he wasn't in danger of dying, he was miserably sick. Back in Missouri Mother suggested that we go and visit and offer what comfort we could. Father thought it over and decided that the trip was worthwhile. The boy was in pain; a visit from the family might cheer him up.

Kansas City's Union Station that July night was like a cavern tunneled out of polished marble. Hurried footfalls echoed off the smooth floor and massive walls. Father boarded the train, inspected our compartment, made sure the luggage was properly stowed, tipped the redcap, kissed my mother and squeezed her shoulder, then shook hands with me. (He was always very thorough about goodbyes.) He would fly out to join us in three days. As the train jolted out of the station, he walked along the platform waving at us as we waved back through the window, his finely molded feet quick-stepping with a dancer's agility against the concrete.

It was my first trip out west. The Appalachians I had seen, but this was to be my first glimpse of the Rocky Mountains. I was curious about them, and a little concerned. I had seen pictures: the jagged peaks, the snow-mantled slopes, the forested valleys; they seemed immense, beyond the capacity of my imagination. They were mammoth and unruly, so unlike the gentle, well-mannered topography of Missouri, with its hills that unfolded in vales and rumples like a freshly laundered towel.

Once the train crossed the border into Kansas (a few minutes after leaving the station), Mother and I made our way to the club car. The interior was soothingly lit with recessed lamps. We settled into corduroy chairs. I ran my finger around the polished rim of a

122

chrome ashtray. A black man in a starched white coat Cities
moved with dignified grace behind a sleek wooden on the
bar. There weren't many passengers in the car. It would Plain
take all night for the train to cross Kansas, and unlike
Missouri, which was Southern, alcoholic, and fun,
Kansas was Yankee, abstemious, and dull. I ordered a
Coke. Mother ordered one, too, and from a mono-
grammed silver flask tucked in her purse, she poured a
healthy measure of bourbon into her glass.

The lights of the little towns west of Kansas City
spattered against the windows like liquid moths. The
roomy car rocked gently back and forth. The black
man replenished our Cokes and looked discreetly
the other way when Mother spiked her drink. After
two drinks she told me about a summer in the 1920s
when her family had traveled by train out to Colorado
Springs to escape the terrible Missouri heat. Her
younger brother—a pale, blond, pigeon-chested
boy—suffered from asthma.

"It was hard to believe he was even sick," she said.
"He always smiled so much. He was such a pretty little
boy. He had beautiful blond hair and blue eyes. He
loved the ride out west. The sight of the mountains
seemed to pump him full of energy. His cheeks took
on color, and he could breathe without difficulty."

Her eyes tightened to little buttons. Her voice
seemed to emerge from a narrow pipe inside her throat.

"It was so sad when he died. We never recovered
from it. He was so charming and good-looking.
Though I suppose he might have been killed in World
War II. He would have been the right age to serve."

I thought of my own brother lying in a Denver hospital, breathing through a tube, his enflamed lungs
wheezing with obstructive particles. Mother's brother
had died of a malady which, in 1955, could probably
have been cured with broncho-dilators, but which

back in the twenties could be treated only by moving the patient to another locale. I remembered thinking how geographic some diseases seem. Malaria in the tropics, tuberculosis in England, yellow fever in the Orient, pneumonia in the Arctic. Later, I would ponder the symbiotic relationship between illness and certain landscapes, but for now, sitting with my mother in the club car of the Burlington train, dressed in a gray suit and red tie, posing (unsuccessfully) as a little adult, I was content merely to wonder if they had jazz clubs in Denver like they did in Kansas City, and if Chet Baker ever played there, or Stan Kenton and Max Roach.

I slept fitfully that night in the upper berth of the little compartment as the train clattered across Kansas. Mother had bundled herself like a mummy in the lower bunk, with the blankets pulled up to her ears. She loved to sleep. She could sleep all day, too, and sometimes she did, much to Father's dismay. She used sleep as she did alcohol, as a means of placing herself beyond the tentacles of her problems. With her head on a pillow or a cocktail in her hand, she seemed perpetually in the act of losing herself in some forgetful reverie.

Toward dawn, with a thin film of light coloring the crack under the window curtain, I swung my feet out over the bunk, crept down the ladder, stole across the floor, and raised the curtain a few inches. Outside it was getting light, a faint, misty light, just enough to outline a flat, featureless horizon silhouetted with a solitary windmill or tree.

But no mountains. I felt baffled and confused.

"What are you doing?"

Mother peered out of the corner of her berth. Her large eyes, myopic without glasses, were glazed with sleep.

124

"The mountains," I grumbled. "I'm looking for the mountains."

"It's too early. You can't see them yet."

"But we must be close to Colorado. We've been traveling all night. Kansas doesn't last forever. Where are the mountains?"

"The mountains are deep inside Colorado," she explained. "Denver is at the foot of them. You won't see them for a while. Now go back to sleep."

I climbed back up to my bunk. The porter had indicated that our route would take us across northern Kansas and southwestern Nebraska to Julesburg, Colorado, on the south fork of the Platte River, 180 miles from Denver. Julesburg. The name had a solid ring to it. It sounded like a town that people had settled in earnest, with the idea of creating not only a thriving community but a monument to pioneer stoicism and grit. Julesburg. With an imagination conditioned by grade-B westerns, I was hopeful of what I might find there. Wide streets with three and four wagons driven abreast amidst a torrent of shouts and cracking whips. Dusty brick and adobe buildings arrayed in stolid file along elevated curbs. Cowpokes fresh off the Texas trails. Fur trappers in greasy leather coats. Cavalry officers bearing bright sabers on their hips. Rowdy drunks tumbling out of bars. Stoic Indians passing like phantoms between the shadows. Women in voluminous skirts twirling parasols.

Just because I lived in a Midwestern town congested with automobiles, governed by Rotarians, and infiltrated by the specter of TV, didn't mean that everyone else did. Surely there was an alternative. Somewhere— maybe out on these plains—there was a city where people rode horses and lived in shacks and settled their differences with their fists and drew water from creaky pumps . . . all those things I knew nothing about but

125

that appealed to me in a juvenile romantic way. Already I was infected with one of the diseases of modern life: nostalgia for a mythical, less-complicated past. Already I was looking for a place where this nostalgia could be fleshed out into living form.

When I awoke again it was lighter in the compartment. The train had stopped. As I slipped down the ladder it started up, slowly, reluctantly, with a slamming of iron doors and a hallooing of voices. Mother didn't stir. Her face was covered with a sheet. I raised the curtain. The train was gathering momentum. The stucco wall of the depot—in sad repair, splotched with cracks and holes—streamed past. A man in a baggy blue uniform, wearing a pillbox hat and a gold chain dangling from his vest, bent over a leather pouch lying on the platform. A window at the end of the depot floated into view, its glass panes broken out. The depot slipped away; a brick-cobbled street appeared, latticed with ugly wires. Cars puttered about; a mail truck with a flat tire stood next to a high curb. The town was devoid of life. *Where are all the people?* I wondered. Granted, it was early, but this was the Pioneer West, where people got up early to get things done.

The uniformed man had looked old and infirm. He had leaned over the leather pouch in an unflattering posture, his knees cracked apart, the seat of his trousers bagging between his thighs like a hammock. Something was gravely wrong here. This was not what I had expected. The town was more of a shell than a real town; it reminded me of one of those cicada shells that in August clung to the tree trunks in our yard. The town wasn't even like a movie set with false fronts and decorative façades; it wasn't like any place that I had ever seen before. It was more like a place with no future and not much of a past, where a person with acute amnesia might enjoy a life of vegetable bliss. The train picked up speed. More buildings fluttered past. Mother

126

groaned and stirred. In a patch of weeds alongside the tracks a dog was solemnly defecating. A sign next to a deserted street crossing at the edge of town read: JULESBURG COLO.

The mountains were disappointing. They were bigger than I had imagined, and several of the summits, even in mid-summer, were covered with snow, but I was curiously unmoved. The last hour as the train sped southwest toward Denver following the south fork of the Platte River, I watched the peaks rise higher and higher through the crust of the plains. Mother awoke mumbling for coffee, and I made my way to the dining car and brought her back a pot. She was dressed and sitting at the window, staring out at the empty land. Her face was puffy and wrinkled, her eyes watery and unfocused. "This will help," she said with an unconvincing smile.

The porter came in to make up the berths. Clutching her coffee cup, mother stepped into the corridor. I stood in the swaying door. "Was that Julesburg we stopped at just as it was getting light?" I asked.

"That's right," the porter said. "It sure was."

"It's not much of a town, is it?"

"Nossir. Prob'ly not in comparison with what you're used to."

He skimmed the sheets off the mattresses and folded the berths back into the wall.

"Have you ever been there?"

"I had to spend the night there once."

"What was it like?"

The porter looked up at me with muddy brown eyes. "Well, there wasn't much to it, young man. There wasn't much to it at all."

I wanted to ask if he'd seen any cowboys or Indians,

but I knew he hadn't and I didn't want to appear foolish. At the same time I wanted him to tell me that he had, that the streets were wide and dusty, exactly as I had imagined. Though I knew they weren't, the image clung to my consciousness like a cat to a screen door.

Meanwhile the snow-capped mountains rose on the horizon. For the rest of the way into Denver I gazed at them with perplexity. Certainly their size and shape were exactly as I had envisioned. But something had gone awry in my head; I was haunted by the memory of the city on the plains. The lifelessness of the place seemed to diminish the grandeur of the mountains. And yet there was something about the emptiness that stirred me. I was confused. The response was not what I had expected. After all, it was the mountains that I had come to see. They represented the real meaning of the West to me—the power, the beauty, the majesty. The town represented something else—what exactly, I wasn't sure.

My mood was grumpy as we rode in a taxi through downtown. On first sight Denver looked more like an overgrown Pennsylvania mining town than a western metropolis. Though the streets were orderly and shaded with cottonwoods and elders, the houses were narrow and angular, reminiscent of those in Appalachia. The light of a pale sun seeped between the office buildings. The air was brittle and thin. I had trouble breathing properly. Mother sat in the back seat with her hands clasped primly in her lap. She wore a silly hat with a spidery net that crept across her forehead. She looked frumpy and rumpled . . . not nearly as attractive as she had the night before in the club car, under the glow of the recessed lights, with a makeshift cocktail clutched between her fingers.

My brother, pale and shrunken, lay in the hospital bed like an empty laundry bag. Mother—never that physically demonstrative—leaned over and kissed him *Cities* on the mouth. I felt a pang of jealousy. The big jerk *on the* had scored again. He was always screwing himself up *Plain* in some odd way, cracking up a car or cutting himself or passing out in a snowbank. His view of love was pathological; he believed that love could only be properly requited when it was appealed to from the depths of an incurable sickness. In the summer of 1944, when I had scarlet fever, Mother visited me every night wearing a surgical mask; she lay in bed and balmed my face with a damp cloth. Could that have been the happiest period of my life? In our family love was a kind of wound that opened and closed as the day progressed, widening under pressure of an un-quenchable ardor and closing just as perversely at the slightest hint of a response. Peering into the wound, you could see bright arteries pumping blood with dogged fury, as if rage were the wisest antidote to sor-row, the only worthwhile cure.

We secured a room in a nearby hotel and for the next three days took turns watching my brother get well. Mother sat in a chair by the bed knitting a sweater; the click of the needles produced a faint tin-tinnabulation like the tap of a woodpecker through a grove of trees. Lusty male voices periodically filled the room as my brother's fraternity pals crowded in; they were filled with a kind of prideful swagger at his having survived the ordeal in the snowbank. The family pres-ence evidently made a difference. A splash of color re-turned to his cheeks. The second day the nurse re-moved the tubes from his nostrils. The emphysemic wheeze of his lungs diminished. He began to laugh and joke in a feeble voice.

The afternoon of the third day Father arrived. At the hospital he took charge in his usual officious way. He demanded to see the attending physician. He instructed the nurses to be more thoughtful. He called out for cleaner linen (he was in the laundry business; he knew about such things). He even gave unwelcomed advice to the custodian mopping the hall floor. The hours dragged by. The light in the room waxed and waned and waxed again. The click of mother's knitting needles persisted like an insect hum. The fraternity brothers entered and exited on explosions of boisterous laughter. Father paced the floor smoking endless cigarettes. I read an Erskine Caldwell novel.

Outside, the mountains cast grainy shadows along the downtown streets. Wherever I went, even to the drugstore for a pack of gum, I was aware of their presence. They formed a solid wall to the west that was impossible to penetrate. What lay on the other side wasn't of much interest to me; steep valleys, no doubt, thickly wooded and full of wild animals, where the sun rarely shined. The mountains might have made my dead uncle feel good, but they intimidated me; I found them forbidding and oppressive. I was haunted by the memory of the city on the plain. Its forlorn appearance had aroused an affectionate longing inside my chest. There was something temporary and insubstantial about it. It seemed to belong to the elements as much as it did to the people who lived there. Unlike the towns I knew in Missouri, it seemed to have the potential to disappear overnight. The wind wheezed through its dry streets like the breath through my brother's sick lungs. It made a kind of music that I had never heard before, but that I wanted to hear again and again.

Around three o'clock the old man and I departed for home in my brother's '55 turquoise-green Chevrolet

130

BelAir. The car was equipped with a continental tire kit; glass packs banded the mufflers, which made it roar at the slightest touch of the accelerator. "A real snatch wagon," father muttered as he guided it through dense, two-way traffic on the outskirts of Denver.

We were late in leaving for a variety of reasons, one of which was the fact that the attending physician did not show up until well after lunch to sign the papers and release my brother. The old man was in a stew. He was always punctual and considered it bad manners to keep anyone waiting. "If I ran my business the way that clunkhead does his patients, I'd be out of money by the weekend," he fumed.

Mother tried to soothe him. My brother sat in a wheelchair like a plastic doll with a bemused smile plastered across his shrunken face. Modern science had prolonged his life, as it would again upon occasion, and he was already thinking about new mischief to get into. I enjoyed watching the old man get riled. He did it almost out of embarrassment, almost apologetically, glaring down at his shoes while he fulminated a string of empty oaths and threats. Basically he was peeved at the idea of being mad, of being made to feel this way by another person; no gentleman ever willfully inconvenienced another.

We finally got under way as the sun was beginning to slide toward the mountains. For the rest of the afternoon we waged a losing race with the long purple shadows that looped out over the broken plains. I was glad to be on the way. I had seen the mountains and walked the streets of Denver, and was more than ready to get home. I stared out at the miles and miles of empty grasslands. The journey on the two-lane highway, with Father driving the entire way, would take twelve hours. I was already bored, and in that self-centered way peculiar to teenagers, I was equally enthralled by the boredom and eager to find a way to dramatize the long hours ahead, to give them meaning and focus.

Masses of buffalo had once roamed this land, though I was aware of that fact, I was more interested in finding (at last) a jazz station that for thirty minutes, before finally sputtering out, played a rousing string of Stan Kenton selections. I bobbed my head and snapped my fingers, a pygmy hipster, bubbling with hormones, at the dawn of a new era of consciousness. The afternoon wore on. The light thickened, gilding the undulant terrain with gritty yellows and golds. Father puffed cigarette after cigarette, nonfilter Camels, with the abandon of a soldier about to enter battle.

Down the road sticky little puddles hovered over the asphalt, letting off vapors that shimmered in the air. I blinked and squinted. "An optical illusion," the old man explained. "It looks like a pool of water out there on the road, but it's not. It's a mirage caused by the heat of the sun."

I thought about the Sahara Desert. I thought about hallucinatory cities forming and reforming upon the horizon like banks of soap bubbles. I thought about spindly windmills and the precarious erectness they represented in a dreary horizontal land. I thought about Julesburg glinting in the sun like a rack of cow bones.

The shadows spread, merging into a solid mass that washed down into the draws and gullies and over the ridges and elevated contours. We were well into Kansas when darkness finally fell, though a glimmer of twilight lingered until nearly ten. Once or twice I turned to look through the back window at the fading profile of the mountains. I was tempted to ask Father to stop the car so I could get out and look at them. No particular reason. Just to say goodbye. But I knew how much he disliked having traffic get ahead of him, and so like a dutiful teenager I kept quiet and instead generated a lurid interior film spiced with images of violence and retaliation.

In north-central Kansas a thunderstorm, highlighted by crackly lightning, lit up the sky. Though it kicked up a swirl of wind, it never really came close but angled off in another direction. Father didn't say much, contenting himself with smoking cigarettes and passing every vehicle he encountered. He drove with a steady, compulsive rhythm, as if eager to get through all this emptiness to the familiar touchstones of his own house and town. You can learn a lot about a person from sitting beside him in a car while crossing Kansas. I would like to say my father was taciturn and moody, but actually he was nothing more than conventionally self-centered. If he couldn't charm someone or attract their charm to him, he wasn't much interested in putting himself out. This was especially true of his family, whom he treated with cordiality and deference but not much enthusiasm. His real energy he reserved for his golf- and card-playing pals.

He could have told me stories to pass the time. He had served in World War II and had had some interesting experiences. He could have asked what was going on in my head, but this was the 1950s when fathers led and children followed, formulating their own underground scenarios. He kept the car on the road and didn't fall asleep, and for that I was thankful. Back then, for a teenager, camaraderie was something that could only be achieved with other teenagers. Fathers were sentinels at the castle gates, and to get their attention you had to club them with a stick or pour boiling oil onto their heads.

I whiled away the time by listening to the radio. Country and western stations flared up for a few minutes then faded away. I gazed out the window at the gloomy, moonless night and thought how lucky my brother was to be ill and in the company of Mother. She liked to talk, and even when she wasn't talking she radiated an air of comfort in her solid presence, the click of her knitting needles, the rustle of the pages of her books.

We stopped several times in dusty towns along Route 36 to eat, drink coffee, and gas up. In one town the filling station attendant knew a mutual friend, which pleased Father; he was forever looking for connections to personalize the network that bound him to the rest of the world. His own world, though small, was farflung; anything outside its immediate influence had little credence or validity. When it came to people he had a club mentality; there were the "right" people, and there were all the rest. As long as he knew enough of the former, the overwhelming number of the latter didn't really matter.

The little towns we sped through, clustered along railroad tracks, nestled under the metallic bulbs of water towers or the cylindrical thumbs of grain silos, were like open-ended chutes through which the wind whistled with unbridled ease. Not even the trees in the tiny parks could provide a focal point around which a proper culture could take root and flourish. Like the wind, like passengers in transit, anything of lasting interest seemed to enter and exit on a fervent rush for mobility. These towns were flimsy and ill-conceived; despite the absence of the buffalo and the Indian, the effortless sweep of the land dictated that it remain unmarked by urban clotting. It belonged to hungry nomads, to migrating birds, to mournful freight trains, to stands of tall grass rippling in the wind.

It must have been several years later, when I was in school back east, that I had my first dream about a

134

city on the plain. I was reading poetry then, and *Cities* the sounds and images of Carl Sandburg and Vachel *on the* Lindsay colored the pictures that illuminated my sleep. *Plain* By the time I entered my twenties, the dream had become an integral part of my personal mythology. It appeared in various guises, though most frequently from the point of view of a car or train hurtling across a flat landscape toward a cluster of spires and towers. There were no suburbs; the city simply began. One moment there was open space, and the next there were buildings and people and congestion and traffic. The road or track dipped under an outer beltway to resurface in a maze of intricate streets. The abrupt transition from open countryside to urban density was the same in each dream. Each dream was softly lit with muted colors. Clouds obscured an afternoon sun that radiated a tarnished glow. The buildings were constructed of sandstone blocks and resembled fortified towers in a far-off desert. As I drew near I experienced a thrill of anticipation. Sometimes the train stopped; other times it ran right through, passing under tall buildings, whipping through dark tunnels, flinging me out on the other side. Unfortunately, the dream always ended before I could reach the streets and mingle with the people. I don't know why this was, but it irked the hell out of me. I belonged inside the city. There were people I wanted to see and who wanted to see me. But whenever I stepped off the train and started up the stairs, the dream sputtered and faded like a projector running out of film.

It took all night to drive back to Missouri. I tried to fill the long hours by counting imaginary birds, by fondling Darlin' Jill's rising beauties, by replaying in my mind Bill Perkins's rollicking tenor sax solos from the Contemporary Concepts album; but the lateness of the hour, the monotony of the terrain, the unrelieved silence between Father and me proved too formidable. It was dark inside the car, and I couldn't even work a crossword puzzle. The night seemed to fold me in a clammy envelope of loneliness. At one point I began to think, Who am I? What kind of man do I want to become? No answers were forthcoming. I thought that I never wanted to live in a town like Julesburg, Colorado, but then again I wasn't sure. There was that music that sounded whenever I thought about the town, and that I associated with no other place I had ever been. The music was sad and melancholy, and it filled me with an inexpressible yearning . . . for what exactly, I did not know.

It was no fun being an adolescent, I concluded with a sigh. And if that was the case, it must be even less fun being an adult.

As we drew closer to the Missouri River, the air grew more humid. Trees bristled along the road. Thunderclouds loomed on the horizon. Lightning illuminated the plodding course of the highway. Around three A.M. I fell asleep to the sound of the wind whining through the window vent. Father was smoking another cigarette, and the acrid fumes filled my nostrils like the scent of a powerful incense.

Blood
for the Sun

We had eaten lunch—discretely out of sight behind
our car—and had just stepped back under the brush
arbor when we saw something that neither of us had
ever seen before. Two men, suspended by ropes pinned
to the flesh above their shoulder blades, were hanging
six feet over the ground. Dark blood trickled down
their backs; their long, glossy hair gleamed like a
raven's wing. Each man clutched an eagle feather,
which he flapped urgently up and down.

A hot August sun boiled overhead. Under the shade
of the arbor other men, clad in T-shirts and ballcaps,
beat drums and wailed in high-pitched voices. A throb-
bing sound mixed with ululating cries floated out over
the tall cottonwood in the center of the circle. From
the topmost branches dangled taut ropes with their

grisly human cargo. A stiff breeze whirling across the arbor kicked up curlicues of dust.

For most of the morning we had watched other types of piercing, mainly involving young men and boys. With pegs protruding from their chests, they had pulled back with all their strength against ropes tied to the cottonwood tree until the pegs popped free. That was absorbing enough, but the two men hanging limply from the branches was a sight we could not comprehend. Though we could acknowledge what was happening, the reasons seemed mysterious and arcane. We were confronted by a spectacle that plumbed the very heart of aboriginal America.

An ancient ritual known as the Sun Dance is performed every summer out on the Great Plains at the Sioux, Cheyenne, and Crow Indian reservations. It is one of the most extraordinary Native American rituals, rivaling anything else on the continent in power and mysticism, including the Hopi Snake Dance and the Yaqui Deer Dance. The one we witnessed took place on the Pine Ridge Reservation of South Dakota, home of the Oglala Sioux.

The Oglala have an interesting history. The largest branch of the Teton or Western Sioux, their ancestry, according to anthropologists, goes all the way back to Tennessee and North Carolina. External pressures in the sixteenth century forced them to embark upon a long migration through the Ohio River valley to Minnesota, where, in the late seventeenth century, they first encountered French traders and trappers. Driven from Minnesota by the Chippewa, they ventured out onto the northern plains, reaching the Black Hills around 1775. During the long struggle against European encroachment onto their hunting grounds, they were led by such warriors as Red Cloud and Crazy Horse. In battles along the Bozeman Trail (1866–68)

138

and at the Rosebud (1876) and Little Big Horn rivers
(1876), they either defeated federal troops or fought
them to a standstill.

The 1880s were a grim time for the Oglala. With the buffalo ruthlessly decimated by white hunters, they were forced to live on reservations where rations could be doled out to them. The Sun Dance was outlawed in 1884, and for good reason. Anyone willing to subject themselves to such an ordeal would most likely find campaigning against the U.S. Cavalry an invigorating sport. And so, like many practices censored by the federal government, the Sun Dance went underground and for nearly half a century was performed away from disapproving eyes in remote pockets of the Pine Ridge Reservation. In 1934, as a result of the Indian Reorganization Act, which established the legality (in white parlance) of many religious activities, the Sun Dance resurfaced, albeit in a bowdlerized version that did not include piercing. In the 1960s—with the advent of the Red Power movement and the corresponding heightening of Indian consciousness—piercing recommenced in earnest.

It is an unsettling spectacle for a *wasicu* to witness. Our Judeo-Christian tradition sanctions martyrdom, but only when it holds out the promise of salvation. Christ suffered fearsome torments on the Cross, but he was finally relieved of his agony by death and the ascension of his body into Heaven. But to suffer physical agony for the living, so that one's people may benefit, is not as comprehensible. And yet that is why, today as in the past, Oglala men subject themselves to the rigors of piercing.

Participation in the ritual is voluntary. Not every man feels compelled to undertake it; a sign or signal in the form of a dream or vision usually indicates a person's willingness. Others participate to give thanks for having survived a crisis. The intensity of suffering forms a deep bond, not only between the dancers, but with the oldest and most sacred tribal traditions. As Arthur Amiotte, a Sioux artist, has said: "Inherent in the Sun Dance itself is the total epistemology of a people. It tells us of their values, their ideals, their hardships, their sacrifice, their strong and unerring belief in something ancient."

The ultimate aim of the ordeal is to bring the participant into contact with Wakan Tanka, the supreme manifestation of spiritual power in the Sioux cosmology. The circle formed by the brush arbor, of which the tree is the center, is a holy and mysterious place. Throughout the ceremony, the circle is constantly purged of evil influences by shamans bearing trays of burning sage whose smoke drifts sweetly over the parched and trampled dust. The cottonwood with its rawhide thongs dangling to the ground provides the focal point for the ceremony. Sanctified by elaborate prayer and ritual, it forms the axis mundi, the tree of life, by which the participants come into contact with the awesome powers of the earth. In effect, the tree functions as a pipe or stem connecting the mortal body to all that is sacred (*wakan*) in the world.

The ordeal is vitally important to Oglala traditionalists. Above all, it is *theirs*, uncorrupted by Christian influences. It is the most compelling antidote they can offer to the negative impact that *wasicu* culture has had on their own; it offers a viable alternative to alcoholism, immorality, and spiritual lassitude. The ordeal is inimitably *Indian*, intensely physical and sublimely visionary, a commitment of body and soul to the preservation of the ideals of the people.

This type of offering has no equivalent in our culture. It can't be satisfied by signing a fat check or turning over old clothes to a welfare agency or doing volunteer work in a soup kitchen; the offering can be *Blood* made only in blood suffering. "The Indian religion is a *for the* hard one," an old man told me afterwards. "It has to *Sun* be. We have faced the threat of extinction for so long that in order to survive we must be as hard as the granite core of the Black Hills."

During a Sun Dance friends and family often will have little pieces of flesh gouged out of their arms. These offerings are then deposited on a buffalo skull to dry in the sun to help the dancer endure the misery of hanging by a rope attached to his body by sharp skewers jabbed through the skin. Blood for blood . . . your blood for mine . . . our blood for the people.

As we watched, one of the young men suspended from the ropes passed out and, like a bag of grain attached to a pulley, twisted slowly in the breeze. A shaman elbowed him in the ribs, whereupon the young man began to beat, feebly at first and then with growing ardor, the eagle feathers clutched in each hand. The weight of his body pulled the pegs away from his shoulder blades in wads of frightfully puckered flesh. Over the dusty, trampled ground he drifted like a curious bird, bound not by any coil to the earth but rather by an implacable tether to the sky. The chanting and drum beats uptempoed from under the brush arbor. Waving his arms wildly, he tried to break free but couldn't. Finally, in a stupendous act of courage, he pulled himself up higher on the rope, and, letting go, spread out his legs and arms like a sky diver. The shock ripped the pegs out of his back with a sound like ripe pears striking a concrete floor.

Two shamans rushed forward, one to rub an herbal compound into the deep puncture wounds in his back.

A few minutes later the man was up and dancing around the brush corral, his face shining with a mixture of agony and exaltation.

We were witnessing the climax of a complicated four-day ceremony, and for the participants the culmination of a long period of instruction and fasting that ends in an apotheosis of blood and pain. Most men subject themselves to the ordeal only once. The wounds inflicted by the skewers are by no means crippling, though they do leave indelible scars. Those men marked on both the chest and back have usually performed the ceremony at least twice. The scars are a special talisman of bravery and fortitude that does not go unnoticed in the Oglala community.

Piercing is more than just an act of self-torture. To the untutored *wasicu*, it seems inconceivable that any human being would voluntarily lacerate himself and then expose his wounds to the elements. The symbolism is complex; piercing provides the means by which the participant opens himself, both mind and body, to everything in the universe that is *wakan*. In an act of bold assertion, he renders himself sublimely passive, thus uniting within himself the male and female antinomies that make up the world.

Historically, young men performed the dance to test their courage and endurance for the trials of warfare at which they hoped to make their mark; today, there are other inducements. One man in his sixties, recently recovered from cancer, had his back pierced in two places just below the shoulder blades. Accompanied by the frantic pounding of drums, he dragged an unwieldy bobble of eight buffalo skulls several times around the brush circle until the weight of the skulls finally tore the pegs out of his back. A woman whispered to me that he was undergoing the ordeal to give thanks to the Great Spirit for curing him of the white man's disease.

Before the dance each participant undergoes lengthy instruction and preparation. Piercing does not usually commence until the third or fourth day; the first two days are spent in fasting and prayer, with the participants facing into the sun and mouthing incantations. Friends and relatives come and go; Indians or family members who wish to demonstrate their sympathy can remove their shoes and join the dancers in the circle. These dancers are vividly clad in tribal costume and form a kind of supporting chorus to the men undergoing piercing. For hours in the grueling sun they shuffle back and forth to the din of drums, tooting shrilly on eagle-bone whistles. Wreaths of silver sage band their ankles, wrists, and skulls. Arms outstretched, palms uplifted, they face into the sun, beseeching the powers to have mercy upon the participants, to give them strength to endure the ordeal.

One ceremony we witnessed that morning involved a boy of twelve. Two circles painted over his nipples indicated that he was to perform. A skirt, beaded around the hem, covered his legs; his wrists and head were circled with garlands of silver sage. Two shamans placed him on his back at the foot of the cottonwood. One bit the flesh on his chest and inserted the skewers. The boy's feet trembled fitfully as the men worked over him. Then they drew him to his feet and immediately he backpeddled away from the tree until the rope went taut. The weight of his body caused the flesh over his nipples to bulge alarmingly; then he dashed forward and placed both hands against the cottonwood in an attitude of prayer. Again and again he repeated this action, each time hurling himself harder against the stiff rope, trying to wrench the pegs out of his chest.

The urgency of the effort was unmistakable. Everyone, young or old, tethered to the cottonwood, must try to release themselves as quickly as possible. Prolonged attachment to the sacred world is tempting but dangerous.

Finally a shaman escorted the boy back to the tree where they prayed together. Then, hooking him around the waist with one arm, the shaman, facing the opposite direction, ran with the boy and, as the rope grew tight, pulled with all his might. The pegs blew out of the boy's chest with an audible pop, triggering a spray of fresh blood. Relieved of his burden, eyes gaping, the boy staggered back into the arms of his family, who swarmed over him with tenderness and concern.

A few minutes later other shamans paraded the boy around the brush corral. There was no cheering or applause, only silence, though most of the spectators rose gravely to their feet. A sort of victory lap like at the Olympics, with no cameras to record the event and only Wakan Tanka and the people as witnesses. The shamans stutter-stepped grimly at his side. The boy's round face was stained with tears. After finishing the lap, he rejoined his family.

To the cloistered eye, the land seems boundless, devoid of meaningful features. It isn't flat—there are other parts of the Great Plains, notably the Llano Estacado of Texas, that are much flatter; rather, it's like a succession of broken slabs, cracked and tilted by erosion into a variety of surface planes. At intervals these slabs warp up into tree-covered buttes and tables, with truncated tops like platforms. Myriad creeks snake down through the draws and gullies. Though bone dry in summer, they conceal a water table that nourishes dense stands of elm, ash, and cottonwood, along with plum and chokecherry thickets.

On hot afternoons cottonwood leaves make soft *Blood* fluttery sounds that delicately overlap one another and *for the* meld into a thick, lathery hum. In the morning cumulus *Sun* clouds stack up over the Black Hills, fifty miles to the west; by midafternoon, propelled by westerly winds, they douse the parched grass of the Pine Ridge Reservation with intense rainsqualls. Lightning forks down from the thunderheads, striking the slopes and occasionally igniting fires.

Scorching in summer, ravaged by Arctic winds in winter, it is a land of extremes, with temperate periods of short duration in between. The Teton Sioux—of whom the Oglala are the most numerous—arrived out here (so anthropologists say) in the mid-eighteenth century. The Oglala think they've been here a lot longer, almost as long as the buffalo, which first emerged from a hole in the Black Hills. In the centuries since, against both Indian and white enemies, the Oglala have fought for this land.

The soaring arch of the sky pulls the gaze up naturally to the clouds. The emptiness cries out for a vision to personify it, a sign or portent that man, insignificant in comparison to all this space, has a purpose and a function. And so for generations Oglala warriors have fasted on top of flat-topped buttes or hung from ropes in an effort to focus the vagaries of their uncertain existence into the radiance of a visionary experience that will unite earth with sky, themselves with Wakan Tanka. At the pitch of their suffering, with the metaphoric grace of poets, they fuse the elements of their harsh lives into luminous wholes. This is powerful country, ageless and unspoiled, redolent with magic, strong as a buffalo heart.

145

River of Thunder,
River of Gold

I.

We didn't get on the river until well after five. Assembling the boats, stowing the gear, pausing to talk and drink a beer took more time than we had reckoned. The San Juan River at Sand Island Campground outside Bluff, Utah, was running at a rapid clip—nearly thirty-six hundred cubic feet per second, according to the note tacked to the bulletin board. Earlier that day, driving through Shiprock, New Mexico, we had encountered several downpours. It was the final week of August, the height of the monsoon season on the Colorado Plateau. Some portion of rain could be expected to fall every day. This afternoon the surface of the San Juan was speckled with sticks and twigs and gritty clots of foam.

There were five of us in the party—four men and a woman. Leonore and Christian were traveling in kayaks, Billy in a Sea Eagle, Donald in a sturdy, inflatable Comanche. I paddled a seventeen-foot Mad River canoe packed with camping gear and supplies. I had paddled other canoes on other rivers, but never through rapids and never this precariously loaded.

Billy and Donald shoved off first. I followed, with the kayakers bringing up the rear. We slipped under the Sand Island Bridge, disturbing a colony of bank swallows that charged in and out of their mud-daubed nests. For the first few miles in the waning light there was little chatter; we were preoccupied with testing paddles, shifting equipment, and refastening clamps and hawsers. After sitting all day in a van it was strange to be floating on a river. Despite its comfortable beam, the canoe felt tippy and precarious.

Downstream from the bridge, the river surged against a tall sandstone cliff, shifting abruptly in direction with a splurge of bubbles. Spacing ourselves generously, we skirted the outer edge of the channel to prevent the current from shoving us against the canyon wall. The sun was rapidly declining; the wall cast a cool shadow across the water. I was momentarily chilled by its touch. Summer was fading from the air. The season had turned and like a mossy turtle was sliding on its belly toward the September equinox.

The valley downstream from Bluff was spacious, filled with pastureland and cultivated fields; the banks were fringed with cottonwoods and willows. To the north lay Mormon territory, to the south the Navajo Reservation. Rising in the rugged pinnacles of the San Juan Mountains of southwest Colorado, the river dips into New Mexico then crosses into Utah near the Four Corners junction. Down from Bluff it carves a twisting path through arid redrock terrain, a wild and scenic country of narrow canyons and bizarre formations, before dribbling out in the static waters of Lake Powell.

Swallows darted over the river. Dragonflies skimmed through the air on papery wings. Out from the shadow of the tall cliff we drifted into a slice of warm sunlight. The current splashed and babbled. Tiny fibers, illuminated by the sun, twirled over the ruddy brown surface. From a ledge on the Navajo side a shaggy raven, solemn as a Baptist deacon, observed our progress with a series of gargling croaks. As we drifted past a small island tufted with tamarisk saplings, there was a loud boom downstream. My heart jumped inside my chest. The sound was echoed by others. "Beaver," Donald called out.

I turned around with a start. I had no idea he was so close. He leaned back against the seat of the Comanche like a man in a rocking chair. The double-bladed paddle lay across his knees. He was outfitted in a tricolored dry suit with a Class III Hi-Float life jacket. A survival knife for cutting tangled lines dangled upside down within quick reach from the neck of the jacket. A pair of sunglasses gave his face a dashing air. "Christian better think about stopping soon," he said. "It's getting close to suppertime. We don't want to be on this river after dark."

The sun had disappeared behind the cliffs on the Navajo side. Behind us, arching over the plateau, rose a canopy of gloomy darkness. It was the moonless period of the month; if we floated much longer we would have only the residual glow of the sun off the sandstone walls to navigate by. As if aware of the urgency, Christian bolted downstream in his kayak to locate a campsite.

A half hour later we guided the boats into a nest of reeds on the Navajo bank. Christian had found a campsite—an Anasazi ruin tucked under the brow of a gaping overhang sixty feet up the face of a cliff. With as little noise as possible, speaking only when necessary, we secured the boats, collected the camping gear, and hacked our way through the reeds and grasses across a rock-strewn wash. The steep cliff gave off a glimmering light; in the moonless air we could barely see where we were going. Donald muttered under his breath. Billy, a heavy-set man in his early fifties with bad knees, panted audibly. Led by Christian, whose pale blue eyes contained a feline gift for detecting objects in the dark, we started up the slope, hauling bedrolls and food. Christian darted ahead, agile as a mountain goat; the rest of us followed clumsily. Halfway up, I banged my knee against a rock and cursed in silken whispers. Leonore mashed her hand on the blade of a prickly pear cactus. She didn't cry out or whimper; in the beam of a tiny pocket light Christian carefully extracted the thorns.

The slope flattened into a shelf that scooped back into the cliff. A moment later the flashlight picked out several ruins. Strewn with rubble, the shelf inched up an incline to the foot of a concave wall decorated with faded petroglyphs. I threw down my gear and waited for my lungs to refill. We were standing in the center of an Anasazi time capsule, relatively undisturbed by outside meddling. An uneasy sensation crept over me with the stealth of a spider. We needed to be careful; what we were doing was patently illegal. Our voices, hushed and cautious, echoed off the arc of the wall and back down into our faces. On an earlier trip, Christian, quite by accident, had stumbled upon the site. Now at 9:30 on a summer night the five of us had breached the premises. I felt a bit awkward at the prospect of spending the night in a ruin dating back hundreds of years. A quick inspection revealed that the shelf was littered with pottery shards and bone frag-

150

ments and minuscule husks of corn. At one time the place had evidently supported a thriving community.

The people had most likely farmed plots of beans and squash in the bottomlands. The climate was wetter then, and big game like deer, antelope, and mountain sheep were plentiful. In the thirteenth century a severe drought lasting for decades had curtailed the water supply; enemies from the north threatened the Anasazi's agricultural life. One day they packed up their belongings and slipped down the cliff and disappeared. In the centuries since, the walls of the claustrophobic dwellings had collapsed to mounds of rubble; the interiors were heaped with sand and dirt and shattered rocks. Next to one ruin lay the outline of a circular kiva. Though limited in size by the dimensions of the shelf, the site must have been of some importance to merit the presence of such a ceremonial chamber.

We stowed our gear on the flattest surfaces we could find and snooped around until we located enough dry twigs to start a fire. The light from the tiny flame flickered off the umbrella-like ceiling and flowered out into a generous glow that illuminated the entire shelf. The light revealed a half-dozen additional dwellings backed up against the wall, plus a cluster of weathered pictographs. Directly behind the fire a line of incised steps, barely wide enough to accommodate the toe of my boot, marched up the wall to a ledge. From this vantage point, munching a hunk of bread gobbed with peanut butter and honey, I gazed down at my companions. The glare from the fire illuminated their faces and hands. Hunched over, picking at their food with their fingers, it was easy to imagine them as hungry Anasazi with swarthy cheeks and burly shoulders. I felt like a spirit hovering protectively over an ancestral scene. Maybe I had been here before in another life,

River of Thunder, River of Gold

squatting in the same position. Probably not, though it was titillating to think so. Two bats whirled through the air in antic circles. Over my head, sequestered in a gourd-shaped nest, a family of swallows rasped in protest against the intrusion.

The acoustics were fantastic. Billy and I spread our bedrolls near the back wall; almost as if we were at water level, we could hear the river slushing along its bed. The shelf functioned as a kind of gigantic receptor of energy and sound. What information these people must have received every night from the wind and stars! There was a practical application as well; an enemy approaching from the river would have had to creep on little cat feet so as not to be detected. We could clearly hear the gurgle of the current, chunks of driftwood thunking against the tethered boats. Voices inside the shelf, even when delivered in a whisper, sounded hushed and confidential.

With the fire doused the stars blinked on like pin spots across a cluttered lightboard. In places they were so brilliantly dense they blurred the configurations of familiar constellations.

"Lots more stars here than when we used to camp out in the backyard," Billy observed.

"Uh-huh."

"You remember the time you got so scared looking at shooting stars you had to go inside?"

"No, I don't."

The night air had thrown a veil of sand over my face. Somewhere to my left I heard Donald unscrew the cap of a water bottle and take a thirsty swig. Christian stretched his legs and cracked his knuckles. Leonore rolled over on her side. Far below, the river frothed and churned.

"Who left the faucet on?" Billy mumbled.

A moment later he added, "I must speak to the management in the morning."

152

II.

We sat for a while on a ledge watching the soft light of the morning steal over the river. A wide valley dotted with trees and shrubs and grazing cattle opened before us. On the Navajo side steep cliffs muscled down to the river; on the Mormon side alluvial bottomlands extended to a line of distant hills. Out in the channel a flock of teals feeding quietly suddenly exploded into the air. But that was the extent of the excitement. A pink glow suffused the brittle air. The valley was muffled in a stillness that made it easy to visualize small bands of Anasazi tilling beans and corn, the smoke spiraling from their cooking fires.

We dawdled in our eyrie for as long as we dared. The expanding light penetrated to the back wall. The shelf was littered with artifacts, but no one pocketed anything. If something was picked up and inspected, it was carefully returned to the same spot. As we packed our gear and prepared to depart, we eradicated all signs of our presence. We disposed of our litter, pulverized the charcoal from the fire, and smoothed out the impressions that our sleeping bodies had made in the dust.

By ten we were on the river. The current was still charged from the runoff of the previous day; the first riffle we encountered was lathery with chocolate waves. The canoe breezed through, steady and responsive. I leaned down and patted her sleek flank.

Christian pulled alongside in his kayak. "The water surprises me," he remarked.

"Why's that?"

"I was worried it might be too low, that along the shoally stretches we might have to drag the boats."

His features were thin and blond. He spoke with a distinct Hungarian accent. In the twenty-five years that he had lived in Albuquerque he had floated all the

153

major Southwest rivers. He was the leader of our little expedition; he chose the campsites and determined the order in which we would run the rapids.

By noon the walls of the river had converged to form a narrow gorge. The bottomlands disappeared, along with the willows and cottonwoods. The steep banks crowded right up against the water. Dreary gray walls soared hundreds of feet into the air. Spiny cactus bristled off the ledges, along with stunted juniper trees. A warm sun beat down; we peeled off layers of unnecessary clothing and smeared on tanning oil. Billy had floated the San Juan earlier in the summer with Christian. "There's enough grit in this water to screen out the flash of a nuclear explosion," he declared, splashing handfuls across his chest and arms.

I had to laugh; with his rotund body plunked down in the Sea Eagle, he resembled an aquatic buddha. His eyes were wide and expressive. Clamped between his teeth was the stem of an unlit pipe.

Near mile twelve we stopped to have lunch. Spirits were high; the pace of the river had invigorated us. We joshed and giggled as we devoured fat sausage sandwiches smeared with Dijon mustard. Leonore looked lovely in her wet suit; long black hair cascaded in glossy coils down her back. Billy told a joke, which had everyone wheezing. As we climbed back into the boats we heard the grumble of thunder. The dark edge of a storm cloud nudged out over the canyon. We paused to listen and watch. The cloud rumbled and swelled.

"A purely localized phenomenon," Donald announced blithely. "It's sprinkling somewhere up on the plateau. It won't affect us."

Nonetheless he opened his river bag and pulled out his foul-weather gear. As soon as we shoved off, the sky thickened, and a fine rain sheeted down against

our faces. At a bend below the lunch spot was a mod- *River of*
est rapid that featured a stack of high-standing waves *Thunder,*
at the foot of the tongue. Christian plunged ahead, *River of*
followed by Leonore and Billy. Rather than skirting *Gold*
the waves, I took them bow-on to test the canoe's response. Up and down we bobbed; the canoe maintained a steady downstream course, shipping a mini-
mal amount of water. Through the rain spilling off my
cap I could see an ugly knot of clouds rolling up the
canyon. It was apparent that Donald's "localized phenomenon" was about to develop into a major downpour.

Downstream, Christian raised the paddle with both
hands over his head—the signal to eddy out. With all
possible haste I steered the canoe to a sandy beach on
the right bank. "It's getting worse!" he shouted. "We'd
better take cover!"

We tied the boats to a flimsy willow tree. I grabbed
my whiskey canteen and hustled with the others up a
rocky slope to a ledge honeycombed with shallow
caves. The five of us squeezed together into the biggest one we could find and watched the sky erupt in a
tumultuous downpour that obscured the cliffs on the
other side. Thunder boomed, lightning forked between the walls in livid crackles. Leonore hid her face
between her knees. Billy cracked a joke, but the punch-
line was swallowed up by a thunderclap. Donald removed the bandana from his neck and methodically
wiped his glasses. Christian rubbed his sculpted lips
with the forefinger of his right hand.

I took a slug of whiskey. The liquid seared my
tender throat. The rapid we had just negotiated, the
deluging rain, the vicious bolts dancing up and down
the canyon sent an alarm through my system. I needed
to calm down, locate my center, settle into a functional equilibrium. There wasn't enough time to medi-
tate or consult a shrink; a few hits of sour mash would

155

have to do. By the time the storm, snarling and fuming, passed on up the canyon, I was relaxed.

That was fortunate, because from the look of the river it was obvious that we had an interesting ride ahead. Down from the cliffs on either side countless waterfalls gushed and tumbled. With little vegetation to absorb the rain, the run-off swept through gullies and washes, over precipices and cliffs. As if inflated by an invisible pump, the river rose furiously before our eyes. The current writhed and foamed. Chunks of debris—plants, limbs, plastic containers—whirled downstream.

Back in the boats we rode this slithery, bucking horse with all the skill we could muster. Each side canyon and wash erupted with a torrent of blood-red water. It was as if the land had suffered a drastic wound that caused it to hemorrhage from every opening. The force with which the river churned downstream was frightening. I slugged back another gulp of hot whiskey, planted my feet firmly in the bottom of the canoe, and gripped the paddle between my fingers. My cap felt as if it was rattling on top of my head like a lid on a pot of boiling water. The river was eager to devour me. Down the convulsive trough between the walls I rocketed, punching the water with the paddle, trying to keep the bow pointed straight. In the frantic intensity of the moment it seemed as if I could hear the river calling to me: "Aren't I beautiful? Aren't I magnificent? Isn't this the most exciting thing you've ever done in your life?"

Pay attention! a voice cautioned in my mind. Mind what you're doing! One false move and you're over, and in this current you'll surely drown!

My heart throbbed wildly. Thank God for whiskey, for the false sense of bravado that pumped through my veins. Downstream, the river seemed to warp and

156

buckle in a succession of lathery, upwelling waves. A cry of alarm escaped between my teeth. The waves rolled toward me, flashing like the scales of a monstrous snake. Billy and Donald disappeared into the troughs. The surface of the water was littered with sticks and chips as if a grove of trees had been shattered by an explosion.

I backpaddled frantically to slow the boat's headlong rush; the effort was futile, but at least it kept me occupied. A moment later the craft rose up on the first high wave, plowed through the foamy crest, and plunged down the backside like a toboggan. My rear end left the wicker seat; for a moment I levitated above the canoe, swiping at the air with my paddle. I sat back down with a crunch and dug the blade into the water. It was critical that I keep the boat pointed downstream so that she didn't broach. Up and down over the waves we soared like a rollercoaster; my teeth seemed to float free of their gums and rattle around my mouth like marbles. And then, as mysteriously as they had arisen, the waves sank back under the surface, and like Sinbad on a whirling red carpet I was flung around a bend into a new portion of the canyon.

At mile seventeen we eddied out to scout Eight-Foot Rapid, our first major obstacle. We climbed to a high point on the Navajo side to inspect the situation. The problem here was twofold: vigorous waves and menacing rocks. In addition there were deep holes, formed by the plunging current. The rapid curved around a long bend, which would require some deft maneuvering.

Christian took each of us aside and discussed our options. When he came to me, he beamed a confident smile. "You did a splendid job in the waves. Now let's see what you can do here."

His voice was calm, his manner relaxed and assured. I was momentarily distracted by the piercing clarity of his blue eyes. The rhythmic lilt of his Hungarian accent was clearly detectable over the roar of the water. In his view my best bet was to hug the inside track of the tongue in order to avoid the rocks to the left. Once off the tongue and into the rapid, I would have to correct my course to the left of center to miss several holes and jagged obstacles along the right bank.

He huddled us together and issued the running order: he and Leonore in the kayaks, followed by Billy and Donald, then me. He explained the rescue procedure in case anyone flipped, then took out his safety rope and tested it. That "anyone" meant me, and we all knew it. Sitting upright in a bulky canoe loaded with equipment, I was a prime candidate to get dumped. As we walked back to the boats, my stomach churned and frothed.

Out in the channel a series of sand waves commenced to roll up the tongue. Despite my nervousness, I watched them attentively. Sand waves are a unique San Juan phenomenon, caused by silt passing swiftly over an uneven bottom. During flooding such as we had just experienced, the waves can reach amplitudes of ten feet. The waves presently out in the channel were only four or five feet high. They billowed up from nowhere and marched resolutely upstream in a procession of smooth ridges. Then, as if by prearranged signal, they collapsed back into the channel.

Christian and Leonore buckled on their life vests, strapped on their helmets, and paddled out toward the tongue. Billy and Donald followed a few moments later, hunched over in their boats, their shoulders canted forward at a tense angle. The river's swift charge created a powerful eddy line, which each boater rode upstream a few yards before cracking across to the tongue. I rechecked the clips and D-rings to make sure the gear was fastened securely to the thwarts and gun-

158

whales. Then I took a nip of bourbon and picked up the paddle.

I slid off the tongue in good form and swept down into the rapid. All around the water seethed and boiled. Up and down over frantic waves I bounced, working the paddle on both sides, struggling to keep the bow pointed straight. Out of the corner of my eye I could see a jumble of toothy rocks rising to my left; hugging the inside track, I bobbed and jiggled around the bend. So far, so good. Water was suddenly everywhere, foaming and splashing, surging against the sides. I backpaddled vigorously, trying to slow the drift. I slapped the paddle down hard, first on the right then on the left, trying to avoid broadsiding a big wave down in the trough. Around the bend the dreaded diagonals appeared; from every angle the waves roared over the gunwhales. Water inside the hull rose to my ankles; the canoe responded sluggishly to my efforts. To the right yawned a gaping hole; bracing the paddle on the left, I turned the heavy bow away from the hole. More diagonals sloshed against the sides; water crept up to my calves. The canoe trembled and shivered; the hull banged as we passed over a submerged rock. As I churned past the spot where Christian had eddied out, he raised his paddle and hallooed in triumph.

There was little time to rejoice. Fed by the continued flow of the runoffs, the river was raging, and down we plunged over additional sandwaves, through foamy riffles, accompanied by unsightly rafts of sticks, limbs, plastic bottles, and bits of styrofoam. At Ledge Rapid at mile nineteen we were moving so fast, the current was so swift, we had no opportunity to pause and scout the situation. By kneeling on the thwart and gaining a little elevation, I could see the tongue veering to the right in the direction of a sandstone cliff.

Billy, several yards in the lead, indicated the path with a jab of the paddle. If I drifted too far that way, the slim cushion of still water between the current and the cliff might not be enough to deflect the canoe's momentum. Under no circumstances did I want the canoe to touch the cliff; the current had carved deep pockets just under the water level in which a dumped boater could easily be trapped. Now I was on the tongue, sliding toward the cliff. For a moment I wondered what would happen if I did nothing. Quickly, I bore down with the paddle on the right side and muscled the canoe away from the cliff toward the inside arc of the current. Safely through the rapid, I put down the paddle and got busy baling.

That evening, we camped a few miles upriver from Mexican Hat near mile twenty-two, with a splendid view of the teetery, sombrero-like formation which gives the little town its name. The pour-off from the furious storm still rolled convulsively, converting the riffle in front of the campsite into a formidable rapid. After running it we had to eddy out quickly. In the process Leonore flipped in her kayak and tumbled downstream, struggling to right herself, with Christian in pursuit. I slipped through the froth without incident then roared into the bank, losing control at the last second and swinging completely around and banging stern-first into Donald's and Billy's boats. Billy was standing on the bank packing tobacco into his pipe. "Nice recovery, Ace," he sneered. I threw my paddle at him.

We dragged the boats onto the soggy bank and secured them to a tree. Christian and Leonore joined us a few minutes later. Leonore was soaked to the bone. Her eyes were buggy with alarm. "It's not much fun riding through a rapid upside down," she yakked in a high-pitched voice. "I kept thinking about all those big

160

rocks and banging my head against them." She un-zipped the front of her wet suit and sprawled across the sand. "I'm so embarrassed. How could I have gone through that raging torrent this afternoon without a hitch, only to get dumped in front of our campground? It doesn't make sense."

"Is this the first time you've flipped?" Billy asked, handing her a beer.

"Of course. It's my first trip in a kayak on a river like this."

"It's a hell of a shock," he agreed. "It's a pretty humbling experience."

"They say there are only two kinds of whitewater boaters," Donald offered. "Those who've flipped and those who are going to." He raised his water bottle in salutation. "Welcome to the club."

We unloaded the gear and set up camp. Once again we were on the Navajo side, this time in a bona fide campsite that encompassed a sizeable plot of rolling bottomland shaded by tamarisks and gnarly cotton-woods. Across the river rose a low, sloping cliff banded with orange and brown sedimentary layers. The layers tilted in a gradual arc that paralleled the river for some distance. Behind the cliff perched the flying saucer configuration of the Mexican Hat. I'd seen it before from the highway, but never from this angle and never up this close. An oblong chunk of sculpted rock balanced upon a neck-line pedestal, it was the oddest formation I'd ever seen in a land where odd formations abound. So uncertain was its equilibrium that a stiff wind seemed capable of toppling it with a tiny push.

A breeze fluttered through the cottonwoods. I hadn't touched dry land since lunch, and now it was nearly seven. It felt reassuring to dig my bare toes into the hot sand and guzzle down a lukewarm beer. The slide and rush of the river continued to reverberate through my body. My legs swayed with a rocking glide. My hands, accustomed to nothing more strenuous than tearing open a brown paper bag to get at the sandwich inside, were bruised and blistered by the bout of strenuous paddling. I held them up to the light of the fading sun. The knuckles protruded like the joints on a bamboo stick. I felt lean and hard. Tested.

III.

During the night Billy awoke to find lying next to him a man with his head completely sheathed in a pair of blue boxer shorts. The night air was damp and cool; before nodding off I had pulled the waistband of the shorts over my head. As I slept I shifted position, and the shorts worked down over my face. Fortunately my nose found the vent in the fly, and I was able to breathe freely. It was this apparition that Billy discovered when he woke up. "I thought you were a ghost," he said. "I thought I had died and gone to hell in a 7-Eleven store that was being held up over and over again by a man in a blue mask."

The morning was flawless. A pristine sky beamed overhead. During the night the flow of the river had abated, and the surface was relatively clean of the debris that had cluttered it the day before.

Leonore stood on the bank drinking coffee, her head cocked to one side.

"What's that I'm hearing?" she whispered.

"The sound of the river," I said.

"No, no. Something else. A bird whistle."

"I dunno."

She pursed her full lips and emitted a tinkly rasp: "Wheep-wheep. Wheep-wheep."

She cocked her head again. "That's not it. Dammit, what is it? Where did it go?"

Gypsum Creek Rapid is located above the town of Mexican Hat at mile twenty-seven. It's not a difficult rapid, but I cheated it anyway, gliding through a smooth passage to the right of a rocky shoal. My companions boomed through the main pathway with a flurry of whoops and shouts. A few minutes later we landed at the foot of a dirt ramp that led up to the San Juan Trading Post and Café. There, at an outside tap, we replenished our water bottles and canteens.

The café was perched on the rim of an overhang. Donald and I squeezed into a tiny booth next to a window with a view of the bridge that crossed to the Navajo Reservation. Directly below, in a foamy swath, the river tumbled through a narrow chute bounded by steep walls.

"I'm hungry," Donald announced.

Indeed he was. He had devoured an enormous breakfast two hours earlier, but the fresh air and exercise had rekindled his appetite.

"I'll have a bacon, egg, and cheese sandwich," he said to the waitress. "No . . . make that two bacon, egg, and cheese sandwiches. And a rootbeer float. Lots of ice cream in the float, please."

Donald generously offered to pay, so I ordered the same thing.

The waitress, a sharp-faced woman with red hair and black eyebrows, glanced up from her pad. "You shoulda seen the river yesterday. The water was so high in the gorge it almost reached the windows."

"No kidding."

"That's right."

"We were on that baby during the worst of it," Donald said.

"You're kidding!"

River of Thunder, River of Gold

163

"Nope."

"And you survived to tell the tale?"

"Four others drowned. But me and him"—he nudged me—"we made it through."

The waitress smiled at Donald. "You look like a real hero. I could use a man like you in my life."

"Lady, you'll have to stand in line. I got offers from all over the country."

Billy crept out of the bar adjoining the café carrying a case of beer. "It's gonna get hot this afternoon," he said sheepishly. "We'll need the fluid."

In his T-shirt and tattered shorts he resembled an aging cherub. His body was round and smoothly muscular. His hair roached up off his skull in a stiff comb of starchy curls. He moved with a rolling, bow-legged gait on a pair of shapely legs, the knees of which had been cruelly battered while playing high school football.

"What happened to Leonore and Christian?" said Donald.

"They're watching after the boats," Billy replied. "You know Christian. He doesn't like to be contaminated by too much contact with civilization during these trips."

"Tell me about it," Donald growled. "One time after a Grand Canyon float he made us paddle the boats eight miles across Lake Mead to our take-out point. Eight miles across a stretch of burning flatwater! I almost died. And this despite an offer from a friendly houseboat to give us a pull. I told him if he ever did that again, I'd sue."

"He can be a real purist," Billy agreed.

"Where there's flowing water you can afford to be a purist," said Donald. "When you run out of current the rules change."

"Sit down and join us," I said to Billy.

"No thanks. I ate last night. I've trained myself to
eat like a snake. If you swallow a rabbit whole on
Monday, you don't have to eat anything for the rest of
the week."

"You don't intend to drink all that beer yourself, do
you?" I said suspiciously.

"No, no. It's for all of us."

Donald sighed. "I'm sixty-one years old and a good
portion of my day, every day, is spent thinking about
food. Crumbs. Biscuits. Seeds. Droppings. Snacks.
Gravel. Whatever's available. The carcass of a stinking
road kill. The cliffs we passed this morning reminded
me of the bread loaves my grandmother used to make
back in Mississippi when I was a boy."

The waitress brought our sandwiches. Donald
slapped ketchup on his and raised the dripping mess to
his mouth. "Ahhh," he gasped.

All afternoon under a radiant sun we drifted through
the Goosenecks, a sinuous canyon that loops back and
forth between drab gray walls. The gradient at this
point was steep, with better than a 6.5 foot drop per
mile. The absence of major side canyons made the ride
virtually rapid-free. There were plenty of riffles, however, caused by rocks flaking off the canyon walls.

Some of the oldest rocks in the San Juan Basin lie
exposed in this section. Dating back 300 million years,
the terraced layers tower up hundreds of feet. Each
layer is composed of countless fossilized corals. A warm
shallow sea once covered the region, containing tril-
lions of tiny organisms coated with calcium carbonate
shells. When the organisms died they spiraled to the
bottom of the sea, where they were buried under other
organisms. Over the eons a crusty reef built up. Eventually the sea evaporated. Mountain ranges shouldered
up then weathered away. Additional seas spread out
over the land. On shuddering tectonic waves the super

continent to which this region was attached 200 million years ago cracked apart, and the pieces commenced to lumber away from one another, a process that is still going on.

At the Goosenecks the river executes an almost perfect double hairpin thirteen hundred feet down in the depths of a mass of sedimentary rock. At one time the San Juan was a sluggish stream that sprawled across a level plain. Then a great plateau was slowly lifted across its path, so slowly that the river was able to maintain its traditional course. It dug into the bed and sawed down through the rising rock creating what geologists call an "entrenched meander." Today, though it retains the winding path of a slow river, the San Juan actually flows quite fast, with an average gradient of nearly 8 feet per mile. That's pretty steep; the Mississippi's gradient, for example, is 8 *inches* to the mile, while that of the Colorado through the Grand Canyon, site of some of the most furious water on the continent, is 7.5 feet per mile.

After the colorful striated walls around Mexican Hat, the dull tint of the Goosenecks was disappointing. Periodically I could smell oil seeping from the rocks. As little as six inches of rain falls per year on the Colorado Plateau, and most of that in intense bursts like what we experienced yesterday. Summer temperatures rocket into the nineties; in winter it can be bitterly cold. With little vegetation, the land stands naked and exposed. All the meat has been carved to the bone by erosion.

The Anasazi gleaned a living from the region before disappearing around 1300 A.D. Southern Paiutes drifted down from Utah and the Great Basin, only to be displaced or absorbed by the Navajo. In 1776 Spanish explorers finally crossed the San Juan. The Americans didn't reach the river until 1859, and quickly retreated. "I cannot conceive of a more worthless and *River of* impracticable region," the expedition leader declared. *Thunder,* Mormon pioneers, in a truly heroic trek, penetrated as *River of* far south as Bluff in 1880. The scent of gold lured pros- *Gold* pectors in the 1890s, though most departed empty-handed. In 1921 the Trimble Expedition mapped the river, primarily to locate the best sites for hydro-electric dams. Additional surveys were conducted in the 1930s. In 1934 Norman Nevills built a boat out of boards from an outdoor privy and floated down the San Juan to its confluence with the Colorado, thus launching the region's current economic mainstay: recreational boating.

As we drifted along I endeavored to halt the meaningless chatter inside my head. The buzz of popular songs, the tawdry images that daily occupy a percentage of my mental activity, seemed totally out of place on the river. (We don't realize what junk heaps our minds are until we experience the solitude of a wilderness region.) To put a stop to it I focused on the color of the sky, the tar-flavored scent of the air, the sparse plantlife sprouting from the gloomy walls, the bench-like tiers that rose from the river in geometric progression. Unfortunately the feat was impossible to sustain. As the canoe bobbed through a riffle at mile forty-six, snatches of a maudlin Christmas song droned in my ears.

One phenomenon that did capture my attention was the sand waves. They are peculiar to the San Juan and appear to be caused by the density and movement of silt in the water. A considerable amount of silt had been washed into the river by yesterday's rain, and as we paraded through the tight oxbows of the Goose-necks we encountered the waves again and again. They were like a kind of mysterious exhalation, vented through the nostrils of the river gods. Spotting an agitation on the surface downstream, and thinking we were about to encounter a riffle, I grabbed the paddle and got ready to maneuver the boat. When I reached the spot the waves were gone. Frequently they billowed up right under me, lifting the canoe on a buoyant swell. A few seconds later they vanished, folding back into the river, leaving a mass of crinkly lines and seething foam.

We camped early that afternoon. The sun was still a good hour above the west rim of the canyon. Donald took advantage of the warmth to give himself a bath. Billy and I elected to remain grimy. Water drying on my face and limbs had formed a solid crust that effectively screened out the rays of the sun. For three days I hadn't bothered to look into a mirror. My legs and arms were the same khaki color as my shorts. I was gradually being converted into a lump of San Juan mud.

The campground was located at the foot of Honaker Trail at mile forty-eight, along a slope that warped up the face of an imposing cliff. Willow, tamarisk, and Russian olive trees provided ample shade; stands of fibery arrowweed sprouted along the bank. I located a dusty patch at the base of a pockmarked boulder, threw out my tarp and bedroll, and plunked myself down with a beer and a cigar. The heat inside the canyon puffed and swelled in a palpable mass which a brisk wind, gliding through the trees, couldn't alleviate. It was mid-afternoon; it felt as though a mangy dog was pressing its sticky fur against my face and chest. It was best to do nothing: lie still, drift off, hanker for sex, fantasize about misty northern fogs. A collared lizard measuring eight inches from nose to tail crept down the side of the boulder. It was banded at the neck with a spinach-green collar that contrasted with a speckled yellow body. "Hello, good friend," I whispered.

The lizard halted and stared into my face. The air sacks under its jaw puffed out in alarm.

"Don't be scared. I won't hurt you."

The lizard gazed at me with cold, lidless eyes. Whether it was impressed with my shape and size there was no way of knowing. With a wave of the hand I could make it scoot, but I wanted to maintain its attention, its regard. It was a glistening, scaly cylinder of specialized impulses, animated by a precise assembly of nerve endings. I could speculate all I wanted and never know more about it than the objective facts of its anatomy and behavior.

Donald shuffled up from the river, clutching his toothbrush and towel. The man was a marvel of coherence, at all times, in any wilderness setting, a civilized, self-functioning unit.

"Hey, Donald," I called. "You know what collard lizards like to eat?"

"What's that?"

"Collard greens."

His face wrinkled with distaste as if I had just farted at the dinner table in front of his wife.

"You know, collared *greens*."

Donald was from the South; he knew what I was talking about.

"Don't tell jokes," Billy groaned from his blanket under a juniper tree. "Write in your journal or read. But don't tell jokes."

Christian and Leonore set up the kitchen and began preparing supper. The sun slipped behind the rim; slowly, like a trough of inky water, the canyon began to fill with shadows. Nearby a canyon wren whistled an arpeggio of limpid notes. The sound took me by surprise. I listened to it awhile before it actually registered upon my senses. Almost before I woke up to its subtle presence, the notes trailed off.

"Leonore! Leonore!"

"What?"

"Listen!"

169

I started toward her then stopped, afraid to move. "What is it?"

"The bird. The bird you heard."

"Yes?" She held a frying pan up to her face as if it were a mirror.

I shook my head. "It's gone now. It's gone again."

She tapped her fingers against the frying pan. "Maybe it will come again," she said with a hopeful smile.

Billy, once a heavy drinker, did not partake of the rum daiquiries; he complained that they were too sticky and sweet. Donald was a teetotaler, and so it fell to Christian, Leonore, and myself to drink the brew. While they toiled away in the makeshift kitchen, Billy entertained Donald with stories of our boyhood in a Missouri river town in the 1940s.

"We weren't raised in your ordinary way," he said. "We were brought up in nightclubs and piano bars. Our parents liked to travel, and they took us with them a lot. They loved to drink and have a good time. They loved to meet new people in strange places and get drunk with them."

"Donald doesn't want to hear this," I protested.

"Donald doesn't mind," Donald rejoined. "Donald wants to hear it."

Billy leaned back against the juniper tree and flexed the fingers of his left hand to work out the stiffness from paddling.

"Every Fourth of July the old man, juiced to the gills, fired skyrockets over the neighbors' houses. It was a hell of a show. Shake shingles on roofs were just becoming popular, and the old man used to aim the rockets so they'd explode in a shower of sparks. He tried to set the whole block on fire. When people called up to complain, he'd invite 'em over for a drink."

"He'd get his ass sued today for a stunt like that," Donald chuckled.

170

"You bet, but back then you could do stuff like that. *River of* One time an actor friend from Hollywood came to *Thunder,* town. The old man hired an ambulance crew to pick *River of* him up at the hotel. The crew marched up to the *Gold* room, strapped the actor to the stretcher, stuck a tube in his mouth attached to a bottle of I. W. Harper, and carried him down through the lobby. The ambulance wailed through the streets to the house escorted by a pair of motorcycle cops. The attendants carried the stretcher up the steps to the patio and deposited it in front of the barbecue grill. The old man handed his guest a fresh drink then pulled out his wallet and paid off the cops and crew."

"Your old man must have thought he was pretty cute," Donald remarked.

"He thought he was the center of the universe," Billy replied.

The contents of the rum punch diminished slowly. I went back repeatedly for refills. By the time dinner was served the shadows rising off the river had chased the last glimmer of light out of the canyon, and I was pleasantly crocked. The four of us—Donald took care of his own needs—huddled around the scorching pot dipping tortillas into the paprika stew. In a matter of minutes the pot was empty. We leaned back against a log and gazed up at the wedge of the sky banded by the silhouettes of the walls. While we were eating someone had thrown a switch, flooding the sky with stars.

"Ahhh," Donald sighed. "We're in tall cotton now."

I can't remember whose idea it was to build the sweatlodge. Things were getting fuzzy by then. With his customary aplomb, Christian erected an oval frame out of wiry reeds and boughs. He scooped a hole in the center of the lodge and lined the entryway with piñon sprigs. There were already several stones baking in the fire; Billy added more. Around the oval frame

171

we then wrapped a blue tarp, packing wet sand along the base to seal off the cool night air. Christian and Leonore hung their clothes on a bush and crawled inside. One by one, balancing them gingerly on a forked stick, Billy carried the glowing stones from the fire and put them in the pit. Christian splashed the stones with water. Steam hissed into the air.

Donald settled on a log by the campfire and pulled out a harmonica. I peeled off my clothes and squeezed inside the lodge. Billy brought a fresh load of stones, which Christian anointed with water. The interior bristled with steam. I broke off a piñon stick and rubbed it across my cheeks and chin. An aromatic fragrance filled my nostrils. Next to me Leonore pressed her face against her knees. Christian tilted back his head and breathed deeply. I thought of the Oglala man I knew on the Pine Ridge Reservation who could call down a shower of pebbles upon the sweatlodge in which he basked. Tiny pebbles clustered around the openings to prairie dog holes, which flew through the air and drummed against the earthen hull with a loud, staccato rhythm.

The atmosphere inside the lodge was ripe with luscious smells. Christian chanted and rapped two bones together. The effect was hypnotic. My breathing relaxed. I seemed to fall into a grassy cradle that rocked lightly over the face of an undulant prairie. From the campfire wafted the sprightly strains of "Oh Susannah." Donald had settled into a groove that might last for hours.

I had no idea how long we remained inside the lodge. Billy brought more stones; the air inside the cramped space thickened and thinned, then thickened again. When we finally emerged, the night air was deliciously clammy against our skins. Christian and Leonore wiped themselves vigorously with a towel and disappeared. I picked my way down the slope, crunched through a stand of tules, and waded into the river. The mushy bottom slurped past my ankles. I yanked my feet free and splashed out further. The current tugged at my calves and knees. I squatted down until I was immersed to the chin. The water was colder than the night air. I was tethered to the shifting bottom by the soles of my bare feet. If I worked them loose, I would be picked up by the current and borne downstream. It was a sure way to die, the fulfillment of every puerile fantasy I had ever entertained.

The whine of Donald's harmonica floated over the river. Billy lumbered back and forth in front of the fire like a hungry bear. No, I would stay right here, thank you. I was a river demon that surfaced at night to spy on campers. I was old and rancid and mantled with scales, and I liked to devour the rubber boats of Outward Bound Expeditions. With a giggle I realized that I was still drunk. "Goody for me," I whispered. "At least I know how to do something right." The river lapped and bubbled against my skin. The surface was speckled with pinpoints of shimmering starlight. A loud clicking greeted my ears. A percussionist was accompanying Donald's harmonica up on the bank. No, it was my teeth; I was freezing my ass off. It was time to seek relief. With a groan I rose out of the water and staggered toward the fire to look for my clothes.

IV.

During the night I was seized by a terrible bout of anxiety. I awoke to find that the position of the stars had shifted and that the segment of sky overhead

173

framed by the canyon walls was partially obscured by drifting clouds. The air smelled of the likelihood of rain. I felt nauseous, as if a wet dog had taken refuge in the pit of my stomach. There was no explanation for it. My response was totally irrational. Lying there, looking up at the clouds, I fretted about having a heart attack. My health was fine. There was little incidence of heart disease in my family; and yet I was convinced that my heart was on the verge of popping like the mainspring of a rusty clock.

I placed my hands on my chest. The pulse was steady, a trifle accelerated perhaps, but then fear has a way of uptempoing the metabolism. This was absurd. There was nothing to be upset about. It was an ordinary night in the canyon. The river slopped and purled. Stars wheeled overhead in awesome gyrations. Granted I had a hangover; my tongue felt like a strip of soiled fur. But I had had plenty of those before; this was something else. The booze, the steambath, the plunge in the river—something—had triggered an outbreak of paranoia. A flock of crows had invaded my consciousness and was hectoring me in spiteful voices. The night was ugly and foul. The canyon was poised like a set of pincers to crush me like a nut.

I groaned and thrashed my feet inside the bedroll. Billy, lying beside me on the tarp, grunted in protest from the depths of his sleep. "Tough shit," I muttered. Billy was my brother. These torments belonged to him as much as they did to me. The blood of common parents pumped through our veins, and yet no two people could be more dissimilar. Physically there were resemblances: the timbre of the voice, the slope of the shoulders, the rolling, cadenced walk. Despite the difference in personalities, the fabric of our bodies was cut from the same genetic cloth.

I fumbled for my canteen and took a swig. The

174

water glided over the oily fuzz on my tongue and down my throat. Odd that Billy, after decades of herculean drinking, had sworn off the hard stuff leaving me, the younger brother, to assume the burden of the family cross. Nearly all his adult life he had labored to drown his demons in booze. It didn't work. It never does. The maggots are impervious to the demands of the most imperial thirst. But he had tried. God knows how he had tried. In his salad days he could drink an ocean of whiskey and still remain afloat.

"Wake up, Billy!" I hissed.

But Billy continued blissfully to snore . . . no longer the hopeless drunk, venting his rage upon an indifferent world, but a mild beer drinker now, toasting the close of a successful whitewater run with a cold brew. At last he had found a way to counter the turmoil of his inner life with a genuine threat from the outside. Danger has a way of lessening the impact of personal conflict. Ah wilderness! In Europe the scions of aristocracy used to fight wars to achieve the same uneasy truce.

I finally fell back to sleep in the clutches of a disturbing dream. A woman in Flagstaff took me into her house and laid me out on a Navajo blanket. With a solution of ocean salt and eucalyptus honey she massaged my legs until they glowed like polished rails. I viewed her ministrations with curiosity. "Now you will be able to walk out of any canyon you want," she declared. She was a handsome, sturdy, self-reliant woman into whose supple hands I would gladly have consigned my life.

Placated by the dream, the crows flew away to a nearby tree. My heart throttled back to its normal tick. The woman continued to massage my leg; I felt we had the opportunity to become lovers of a sort I couldn't begin to define. The next thing I knew

175

was the smell of coffee wafting from the fire outside Donald's tent.

V.

It wasn't until after my second cup of strong Mexican coffee that I felt well enough to move around. A band of sunlight was slowly descending the canyon wall across the river, compressing the last shadows into a compact layer along the tree-lined bank. I found a comfortable spot near a patch of arrowweeds and plunked myself down. The river hissed at my feet. Over this sound, with the delicacy of dogwood petals fluttering to the ground, came the call of the canyon wren. I caught my breath and looked up. Leonore, standing a few feet away, nodded eagerly. She clasped her arms around her chest and stared down at her bare feet. The notes, subtle and evocative, died away on a puff of air.

"That's what I heard the other day,."

"Takes your breath away, doesn't it?" I whispered.

She stared across the river. "It's like . . . I don't know. It's like that's why I'm here. The main reason I came on the trip, I think, was to hear that voice."

The morning air was sweet and mild. We were reluctant to pack up and leave. Billy and I drifted around the campsite drinking coffee and nibbling whatever food we could find. Leonore shared her coffee cake. Donald fixed a heaping stack of blueberry pancakes on his single-burner stove and drenched them with syrup. Billy and I hung around like a pair of jackals until Donald finally took pity and tossed us some scraps. "You guys are the worst moochers I've ever seen," he growled.

The sky between the canyon walls glowed with a

slick enameled glaze, almost as if it had been fired in a kiln. Around nine the sun broke over the cliff behind us, spilling a hot yellow light onto the river. The surface glowed like a vein of liquid ore. The shadows lurking on the opposite bank evaporated under the revelatory touch of the sun. The canyon was opening itself to the advancing day like a clumsy stone flower.

During the night the river had dropped nearly a foot. Provided there was no additional cloudburst, in another twenty-four hours the river would most likely resume its normal depth for this time of year. The flash flood we had ridden through had actually been a lucky boon. In late August boaters usually have to drag their crafts over sandbars and shoals. The wilderness portion of the San Juan River is bounded by dams—upriver by Navajo Dam in New Mexico, which regulates the rate of the current, and downstream by Glen Canyon Dam, which impounds the flow of the Colorado River and backs it up past the confluence of the San Juan, all the way to Grand Gulch Rapid. During our trip rain must have fallen consistently in northern New Mexico, prompting the engineers at Navajo Dam to release water from the reservoir; that, coupled with the run-off from the tumultuous downpour the second day, had kept the current churning at a brisk pace.

We finally put on around ten and started downstream. An hour later the air warmed up, and we peeled off sweaters and paddle jackets. The sun stood boldly between the canyon walls, blazing into every cranny and nook. My mood was bubbly and playful. The furies of the previous night had fled into the dour rocks. The light flanging off the turbid river sparked mischievous thoughts. I slipped in behind Billy and drenched him with a whack from my paddle. "Whore!" he shouted and splashed back, with such vigor he nearly rolled out of the Sea Eagle.

We lunched on a sandstone ledge smoothed and

buffeted by the swell of the river. The canyon was like a chute, and before the dams were built the water level fluctuated wildly, rising in the spring high up the walls before lapsing in late summer to a trickle. Unchecked by man-made obstacles, the river gushed through the canyon at a healthy clip, scouring the banks of litter and debris. Today, in the wake of a steadier current, the sandbars have widened and additional plantlife has taken hold. Species like tamarisk and Russian olive, introduced to the Southwest a century ago, proliferate on every bank and ledge.

Lunch consisted of sausage and bagels with cream cheese and mustard, augmented by peanut butter and honey, washed down with beer and soft drinks. We were huddled under the silhouette of a twisted juniper that pronged out from a crack like a spindly umbrella. The sun beat down against our heads. Powdery, snuff-like dust had settled into the creases of Christian's ascetic face, accentuating the knobs and angles. I'm not sure who heard the sound first, but I saw the bagel in Donald's hand pause halfway to his mouth. A moment later the doleful sound of a saxophone came winging along the canyon walls. Around the bend drifted a raft . . . a fourteen-footer, reinforced with a steel frame, stacked high in the stern with gear. Perched amidships on a plastic seat was a mustachioed fellow in a camouflage hat, who paddled the craft downstream with leisurely strokes from a pair of sweeping oars. Standing on the platform athwart the bow was a brawny, red-bearded man dressed in khaki shorts and a safari jacket with the sleeves trimmed off. His forehead and nose were shaded by the brim of a pith helmet. Between his fingers he clutched a tenor saxophone, from which poured forth the strains of the sultry ballad "Body and Soul." The lush notes spiraled out of the gleaming horn and splashed against the walls. The canyon amplified the sound and sent it rolling back and forth across the river. We gaped in astonishment as the pair drifted past. The bearded man never looked up. His eyes were closed, his cheeks puffed out like a frog's, he was lost in his own little world. The oarsman nodded cordially in our direction. He looked about as relaxed as you might want anyone to be on a river of this magnitude. The raft slipped on downstream. The brooding melody lingered in the air for some time after the two men had disappeared around the bend.

That afternoon we emerged from the Goosenecks into a less winding section where the river ran straight for long stretches. The gradient was precipitous, with the river dropping in elevation over 8.5 feet per mile. Riffles were abundant, and we bounced through one after the other. Around two o'clock we hauled out to inspect Government Rapid, located between miles sixty-three and sixty-four. As world-class rapids go, it wasn't all that daunting, though it was certainly the most formidable we had yet encountered on the San Juan.

The tongue flowed toward a nasty hole and a line of sharp rocks jutting out from the right bank. At the hole the current made an abrupt turn to the left into a mass of high-standing waves that frothed and lathered in a straight line to the next bend in the canyon. Midway along there was another hole, cobbled with smooth rocks resembling the backs of bathing hippos. At all costs this obstacle had to be avoided. The plan was to position the canoe in the center of the tongue and skirt the first hole, then swing the bow around in a forty-five—degree arc and latch onto the long, tumultuous ribbon of waves, making sure to avoid the second hole on the left.

On paper it was a cinch to graph.

Christian and I stood on a rock overlooking the rapid discussing my options. Christian's accented voice was calm and reassuring. The man had a way of making everything sound okay. I found myself agreeing with whatever he had to say. He made sure I understood the route I was to follow, the holes to avoid, the rocks to miss. He spoke softly; despite my nervousness I had no trouble understanding him over the roar of thousands of tons of water crashing against a slew of rocks. "Not to worry," Christian declared, patting me on the shoulder. "You'll do fine. Under that staunch Anglo-Saxon hide beats the heart of a true French *voyageur.*"

Earlier in the summer, near Split Mountain on the Green River, I had flipped in a Sea Eagle while charging through a rapid similar in size and ferocity to Government. The boiling current sucked me down a few seconds then spit me back up. I gulped frantically and disappeared again under the waves. I tried to shove my legs out in front, and promptly whacked both knees against a submerged rock. The pain was intense. I groaned and swallowed a mouthful of water. In front of me bobbed the empty Sea Eagle. I snatched for the grabline, missed, snatched again, and finally caught hold. I swung my legs around the rubbery stern then leaned back against my lifejacket and rode the rest of the way through the rapid, gasping and sputtering. I finally crawled ashore a half-mile downstream, collapsed on the rocks, doubled both hands into tight fists, and thought about puking my guts out. For a long time my heart jerked inside my chest like a pogo stick.

And now I had to face Government Rapid.

Leonore sat on a slab of driftwood watching the river writhe and foam. The straps of her wet suit dangled to her hips. She had a brush in one hand and was moving it up and down the length of her long black hair. She didn't look up when I sat down beside _River of her. "Why do I do this to myself?" she said in a fluty *Thunder,* voice. "Why do I put myself in these situations? Chris- *River of* tian says I can walk it if I want to, but I can't do that. *Gold* He's my kayak instructor. What kind of a vote is that? I've got to tough it out on my own. I feel shitty. I feel worse than I did before my first piano recital. I have to go to the bathroom real bad."

I put my arm around her shoulder. It was then that I noticed how lovely her eyes were. Their blue-gray color contrasted pleasantly with her fair skin and un- ruly hair. They were rimmed with delicate black halos which set them off in their sockets like a pair of oval frames.

"Yeah, it's bad, all right. It's the worst feeling in the world."

"Why do people do this to themselves? I feel like dying."

"'Cause it feels so good afterwards," I said. "After you've made it through and you're standing on the bank looking at the water again."

"There's no logical reason why any thinking human being would subject himself to this agony."

"There's the rush," I added. "Don't forget that. White- water junkies will go to any lengths to experience the rush. It's a kick. It knocks you on your ear."

"I don't care. It's silly. I don't want to do it. I've al- ready flipped once in this river. I don't want to flip again."

I was about to suggest that maybe we walk the rapid together when Christian appeared. His lean, gentle face was composed into a solemn mask. "Are you ready, Leonore?"

"Yes!" she barked, leaping to her feet and pulling the straps of the wet suit over her shoulders. She stuffed the hairbrush into her day bag, snatched up the helmet, and jammed it on her head. "I'm ready, goddammit! I'm ready right now!"

Billy was standing nearby. "Christian gets too cerebral sometimes," he muttered. "You can discuss this shit to death. You scope the rapid, pick a route, get on, and do it. The moment of truth ain't in the discussion. It's in the action. It's what you do on the river that makes the difference."

I watched with mounting trepidation as Christian and Leonore raced through the rapid in their kayaks. Billy and Donald followed. I marveled at Billy's taut posture, the purposeful way he leaned forward in the Sea Eagle. The paddleblades flashed rhythmically over his head, trailing droplets of water. Donald drifted perilously close to the rocks in the Comanche. He kissed the first with his bow, swerved sideways, corrected the drift, levered the paddle on both sides with his strong arms, and barely missed the big hole. Flailing the paddle like a windmill, he bounced onto the ribbon of writhing diagonals that cascaded downstream.

Back on shore I checked my belts to make sure that everything was secure. Then I checked to make sure that my life jacket was properly hooked. Then I settled my ass on the seat of the Mad River Canoe, muttered a short prayer, and shoved off. My stomach fluttered like a spastic wing. I reached the tongue and swung the canoe onto it. I clutched the wooden paddle with all my strength and planted my feet squarely on the floor.

The plan was to cling to the outer rim of the tongue in order to leave ample room to counteract whatever tendency the current might have to force the canoe toward the first big hole. The roar of the water crashing through the rapid was deafening. A moment later the tongue dissolved into a lather of brown waves that slanted down toward the hole—deeper and more

182

menacing, I realized, than it appeared when observed from the safety of shore. I slapped the paddle down on the port side to swing the bow away. The muddle of cross-currents held the boat stationary for a long, suspenseful moment. Then the boat tipped precariously toward the hole. I leaned hard to the left, alternately bracing and stroking the blade; a trio of rocks raised their angry heads through the foam. Water gushed into the canoe; the stern sagged alarmingly. The canoe was in danger of swamping. Water lapped the gunwhales; with the added weight the craft was difficult to maneuver.

And then I looked up. The canoe had proven itself to be sturdy and reliable, but now I realized that it was also smarter than I. The hole slid away off the stern; by some miracle the course correction had been achieved, and there I was, smack in the middle of the channel, racing away from the first hole and positioned just far enough to the right to avoid the second. The canoe bounced over the choppy waves like a leaf in a storm. My ass floated off the wicker seat and slammed back down, forcing the air from my lungs. Up and down the canoe caromed over the crashing waves. Water swirled to my calves. I swiveled my hips and dipped my shoulders to counteract the charge of the diagonals. The canoe maintained a steady course. The diagonals roared against the bow; the canoe bucked and shivered and pitched. Then the force of the water died down; the thunder of the current dwindled to a moderate flow. "I'm through!" I moaned deliriously. "I'm really through!" Billy and Donald, eddied out on the right, rescue ropes in hand, cheered my passage.

There was a final rapid to negotiate, Slickhorn, before we could haul out and camp. It was located a few miles downstream from Government. By this time it was late afternoon; the south bank was shielded by a towering cliff, which blanketed the rapid in filmy shadow. Fortunately it wasn't as strenuous as Government; there were several holes to avoid, plus a narrow, tilted rock that protruded center-channel. Christian strayed to the right of the tongue in his kayak and rammed into a high-standing wave. I was following his progress through binoculars from the bank; for an instant, as he collided with the wave, he seemed to stop dead in his tracks. Something lodged in my throat. The power of the river, its undiminished splendor, revealed itself at that instant. Billy, standing next to me, let out an incredulous "Jee-suss!" Christian disappeared; the next moment the water erupted in an explosion of sparkling crystals, and he emerged on the other side, head down, eyes closed, pumping his paddle with exhilaration.

Once past the rapid we had to make a quick turn to the right to reach the bank. Leonore got through the rapid fine, but in stroking for the bank she flipped and turned turtle and promptly bailed out. Christian caught up with her before she drifted too far and ferried her the rest of the way to shore; then he took off downstream to retrieve the boat and paddle. She was a woebegone sight when the rest of us arrived—wet to the bone, her nerves shot, disgusted and angry with herself. "This sucks," she fumed. "This really takes it in the ear. I seem to tip over in all the places I'm not supposed to."

The campsite was nestled on a ledge shaded by trees and shrubs. The ledge rose several feet out of reach of flooding water. The vegetation was diverse and solidly entrenched, the soil less sandy in composition. Billy and I picked a spot and tossed down our gear. Leonore dragged herself to the cooler and popped open a warm beer. Donald curled an arm around her shoulder and gave her a hug. Slickhorn was the final rapid we would face; tomorrow, it was nothing but riffles all the way through to Grand Gulch and the take-out point.

An hour later, stripped to a pair of shorts, I poked about the campsite. Mouse tracks like tiny hieroglyphs were inscribed everywhere in the hot yellow dust. Clumps of Mormon tea shot up from the grass. Boiled into a liquid, the tiny, bamboo-like stalks serve as a stimulant to the heart. I plucked a handful of juniper berries and mashed them with my thumb; the scent against my nose was tangy and aromatic. Backed up against the pitted face of a rock, spilling into the air in a profusion of silky leaves and petals, grew a stand of datura . . . or locoweed, or moon lily, or devil's apple, or any of the half-dozen names by which it is known. The floppy, pale white blossoms gaped open in the shadowy light. Datura are wary of direct contact with the sun and usually open their petals only at night. Every part of the plant contains a powerful chemical called atropine, capable of inducing violent hallucinations when eaten in the wrong quantities.

That evening we bathed (Billy and I finally relenting) in one of the pools scraped out of the solid stone terraces that rise over Slickhorn Gulch. We climbed up several tiers, each more denuded of vegetation, passing one or two glittery pools, before arriving at a suitable one maybe half the size of a tennis court. Cataracts tumbling from the heights of the plateau had notched deep grooves in the rim of the slickrock; water had then collected in the shallows and depressions on the lower surfaces. Dense and opaque, the pools absorbed the sun's rays during the hottest part of the day; at night they seemed to give off a rusty glow. "Swimming holes on Mars must look like this," Billy remarked. He slipped out of his clothes and planted one foot gingerly on the slimy bottom. His limbs and beefy chest were plastered with silt and grime. Clutching a bar of soap, he advanced deeper into the water. "It's time to lather my fudgies," he announced.

The sun had long since disappeared; darkness began to gather at the bottom of the canyon. The walls that reared up behind us were as bare and scaly as a buzzard's neck. The air was tinted an eerie russet color. We bathed hurriedly, exchanging comments in guarded voices. The site was not conducive to highjinks. There was something spooky about it. The lifeless water was gritty with particles. When I emerged I was coated with a fresh coat of grime. A shiver rippled up my spine, and not just from the touch of the cool night air. I was relieved when we finally returned to the campsite and the familiar props of trees, bushes, and grass.

After supper it threatened to rain. A few sprinkles fell, but the clouds soon crept away, revealing a swatch of night sky crinkly with clusters of stars. We settled around the fire and listened to Christian tell the story of his escape from Budapest after the collapse of the 1956 uprising, and the convoluted and frequently funny circumstances that brought him to Albuquerque. He spoke slowly, choosing his words carefully, fashioning a narrative that, for all its originality, was typical of the fate of political refugees everywhere. His story, fortunately, had a happy ending.

"These river trips always end too soon," Billy sighed. He poked the flames with a stick. A shower of sparks danced into the sky.

"I tell you what I want," Christian said. "And what I intend to spend the rest of my life looking for."

The light from the flame illuminated his chiseled features, casting the hollows and creases into contrasting shadows.

"I'm looking for a river that will last the length of an entire summer . . ."

186

"Amen, brother," Billy muttered.

"Maybe somewhere in Siberia I'll find it, but it's out there, and it doesn't have any dams straddling its width, and it rises and falls according to the dictates of the seasons, and it's wild and ferocious in parts and sweet and gentle in others. It owes allegiance to no one. It is utterly independent of everything except its own primitive force."

"Let's go there," Billy said eagerly. "Let's go there tomorrow."

Donald had fallen asleep under the stars and was snoring blissfully.

VI.

Christian and Leonore departed early the next morning to paddle down to Grand Gulch Canyon at mile seventy and hike up a side ravine. Donald, Billy, and I lingered over breakfast. It was twenty miles to the take-out point at Paiute Farms, and we were in no hurry to break camp. It was our last morning on the river. Tomorrow we would be someplace else, back in Bluff or on the way to Albuquerque. The air was fresh and limpid. A mockingbird gurgled in the bush. A breeze drifted through the campsite carrying the smell of sun-baked stones from somewhere high overhead.

I took my time packing the canoe. I had the routine down by now, and I enjoyed making sure that the load was properly balanced and secured. Since I had the biggest boat I carried the most gear, which had come in handy as ballast.

A pleasant reverie stole over me. Christian's comment about finding a river that lasts the length of an entire summer must have nibbled away at my subconscious, for suddenly I had a vision of following the San

Juan into the Colorado, the Colorado through Grand Canyon, then down the long seam dividing Arizona and California, to the delta at the top of the Sea of Cortez. And then navigating the length of that shallow gulf, skirting the stony shoreline of Baja California, past Isla Angela de la Guarda, past the villages of Santa Rosario and Loreto, past Bahia de la Paz, finally to the rocky headlands at Cabo San Lucas. The trip would take weeks, months. It would take longer than a summer, it would take a year, several years, a decade maybe, the rest of our lives. By the time we reached Cabo we would be doddering and gray. Our children would be grown, our wives would be dead, our names would have been forgotten back home. The stock market would have fizzled, the Japanese would have bought out the major corporations, the Arabs would own all the casinos and resorts, the Chicago Cubs would have won the World Series twice in a row. Like a band of migratory Rip Van Winkles, we would fall asleep in our boats, lulled by the slapping of waves and the incessant, onward motion, and when we finally woke up and staggered ashore, the world would be fleshed out in bright new colors. Indians would greet our arrival with food and gifts, hungry bears would prowl the hills, otters would frolick in the offshore kelp, there would be no sign of Spanish sails anywhere on the horizon.

Below Slickhorn Rapid we encountered several riffles, and then the water settled down to a steady, uninterrupted flow. The gradient between Slickhorn and Grand Gulch was steep—11.6 feet per mile, the steepest we had seen so far. All rivers flow downhill, but this one visibly slants; like the blade of a knife tilted against a crust of hot dough, the San Juan cuts down through layers of ancient rock in quest of the sea.

By mid-morning the sun flooded the long straight

length of Grand Gulch Canyon with yellow light, and the walls glowed with ruddy splendor. The band of cloudless sky between the rims was as smooth and slick as a ceramic bowl. The river gurgled playfully as a sparkling light danced across the surface. Donald, drifting in the Comanche a few yards away, was engulfed in a cone of radiant beams. The clasps of his life vest, the dial on his watch, the lenses of his glasses spangled in the morning air. He resembled the legendary cacique of El Dorado, bedecked with jewels, his bare flesh dusted with particles of gold. He raised his arms, tilted back his head, opened his mouth, and let out a ringing laugh that mingled with the jubilant purl of the river. In the future, whenever I might need an image of animation and vigor to lift my sagging spirits, I would recall this moment . . . Donald's shining profile, the incandescent sun, the river of gold that frothed and sputtered like a liquid meteor.

River of Thunder, River of Gold

Unfortunately the euphoria didn't last. We were running out of river. An hour later the face of the water began to alter. The current slowed; the ripples that agitated the surface sank into a lethargic pool. Sandbars nudged into the air. Rounding a final bend, I had difficulty locating the thread of the channel. Back and forth between the walls I shifted the canoe, trying to latch onto the last sliver of running water. The red cliffs of Grand Gulch Canyon dwindled to a row of modest bluffs. The sky expanded to a yawning arc. Swallows darted across the surface. What was left of the canyon stretched in the distance to a cluster of dung-colored hills. Halfway there, the current petered out.

I exploded with rage. I beat the dead water with the paddle blade. "Where the hell's the river gone?" I screamed.

Billy stole up behind me. Despite the battered fishing hat shadowing his face, his nose and lips were cracked and peeling from the sun. "We're in deep shit now," he croaked. "We got to paddle six more miles to Paiute Farms. And we ain't got any beer left to drink."

I knew well enough what had happened. At the foot of this five-day descent through scenic plateau country lay the quiescent, putty-like wastes of Lake Powell. Impounded by Glen Canyon Dam forty miles to the southwest, the water of the Colorado River backs up past its confluence with the San Juan all the way to Grand Gulch Canyon. Buried under thousands of tons of water lies Glen Canyon, "the most serenely beautiful of all the canyons," according to Wallace Stegner, who floated it in the 1950s before the dam was closed.

I felt my gorge rise with sullen resentment. I had conceived a smoldering hatred for this body of water one afternoon several years earlier. In a small aircraft I had flown from Lees Ferry to Page, Arizona, and from there past the west slope of the massive dome of Navajo Mountain. I spotted the puny impediment of the dam wedged into a narrow slot at the foot of Glen Canyon. I saw the power plant at Page with its smokestacks belching forth clouds of particulate steam. To the north, glistening in the sun like the scales of a dead fish, spread the waters of Lake Powell. (Lake *Bowell*, someone once scratched on a signpost outside Bluff.) Down through the translucent surface I could plainly see the outline of the narrow canyon twisting through the depths like a ghostly snake. Submerged under hundreds of square miles of torpid water were artifacts and pictographs and granaries and ruins; submerged also were some of the most exquisite canyons in the world . . . spectacular formations gracefully sculpted out of malleable rock over millions of years, subtle folds and slit chasms and slender abysses and smooth declivities. The spectacle made me sick. It was like looking down through a foggy glass at the remains of a legendary hero and trying in vain to recall his features, the sound of his voice, the significance of his deeds.

I fumed and muttered and swore. I whacked the paddle against the water and kicked the inside of the canoe. "You bastards!" I roared. "You goddamn bastards!"

"You better stop bitching and get to paddling," Billy urged. "We got a long way yet to go. Every hour we're late after four o'clock we got to pay the pickup drivers eighteen bucks apiece."

I put my head down and stroked the paddle. Two licks on the left, two licks on the right. At the end of an hour we'd covered barely a mile. There were five miles left to go. It was now two o'clock. If we reached Paiute Farms by seven we'd be lucky.

Near the mouth of Grand Gulch Canyon, Christian and Leonore overtook us in their kayaks. The sun beat down against their blistered faces. "The fun's over," Christian muttered with a hopeless shrug. "It's nothing but forced labor from here on."

I took a swig of tepid water from my canteen. Billy and Donald clustered around. "Come on, guys," Donald chided. "We got to pay our dues for all the fun we've been having."

"This is more like the national debt," Leonore remarked, staring out at the harsh metallic expanse of the lake.

A half hour later, at Clay Hills Crossing, a stiff wind kicked up from the south, blowing smack into our teeth. Images of the ordeals of Sisyphus flashed through my brain. I thought of worker bees, cottonpickers, the faceless slaves who dragged the heavy stones to construct the pyramids. It was time for an extended out-of-the-body experience. I stared down at my feet, dug in with the paddle, and tried to abstract my thoughts into a meditative trance.

191

"INCOMING!"

Something struck the river bag lashed in the bow and fragmented with a splat, spraying water against my face and chest. A second object whistled past my ear and plopped into the lake. I looked up. Billy was kneeling in the Sea Eagle swinging his paddle at a rubbery missile winging toward him from a blue cataraft floating a short distance away.

"Hostiles at one o'clock!" a voice boomed through a bullhorn. "Battery number two load up! Fire at will!"

A half-dozen people onboard the cataraft scrambled around under a canopy fitting bloated condoms into slings fashioned from surgical tubing and flinging them at the members of our little party.

A projectile detonated against the hull of Christian's kayak with a loud whump. He started to swear then caught himself and laughed uproariously.

"Bullseye! Bullseye! Target accounted for! Reload all batteries! Sink the Bismarck! Death to the Hun!"

The man barking through the bullhorn was dressed in a pink tutu. Soggy with beer and wine, the skirts drooped over his flabby hips. A sizeable gut paunched over the folds. His sunbaked chest was bare and matted with frizzy gray hair. The tip of a scraggy beard dangled between his nipples. Over a balding skull was a pair of women's panties with twin pigtails sticking through the leg holes. In one hand he clutched the bullhorn, in the other a can of Budweiser.

Stenciled across the pontoons of the cataraft in faded letters was the caption "FLOAT AND BLOAT." Behind their leader the crew scrambled frantically, tearing open plastic packets, pulling out condoms, priming them with beer and water, placing them in the slingshots, then catapulting them through the air.

"Surrender or die!" the man roared. "I want the woman brought to my cabin! The rest of you will be castrated and forced to row the length of Lake Powell!"

Christian was laughing so hard he nearly tipped over the kayak. "What the hell are you doing here, Grog?" he shouted.

"Enjoying a pleasant outing with my buddies."

The buddies, a scruffy, shirtless band of louts, sported ballcaps and cowboy hats. One of them was tattooed heavily on the arms and shoulders. They seemed to be having a pleasant time. They howled and snorted and fired off another salvo of condoms.

"Cease firing!" Grog bellowed through the horn. "Christian, you wretched Hungarian wetback, is that you?"

"Si. Si."

"I'm the self-appointed guardian of this fair lake, so it won't be drained by dedicated Boy Scouts like yourself. Someone has to defend the honor of the flag. There are subversives everywhere."

"Listen here," Donald piped up. "I don't think it's funny. You could hurt someone with those bombs."

The crew hooted and razzed. A chorus of lipfarts filled the air like an insect hum.

"Condoms!" Grog roared through the horn. "Bags! Sleeves! Rubbers! We have a duty to prevent the spread of AIDS to the fish in this pond!"

He lowered the horn. "Christian, where did you pick up this mouse?"

"It's been a long trip, Grog. Which direction are you headed?"

"Paiute Farms."

"So are we."

"Give me the woman to ravish and I'll give you a lift. We got thirty-five horses on the back of this barge. You don't look like you're all that keen to paddle the distance to Paiute Farms."

"We're sure as hell not," Billy declared. "It's hot.

River of Thunder, River of Gold

We're tired. And this flatwater stinks."

Christian looked around. He was in a quandary. He wanted to finish the trip in a natural fashion by paddling to our destination. Unfortunately we had run into an unnatural obstacle: Lake Powell.

"What do you say, mates? Do we throw in with this rogue?"

"Yes! Yes!"

Donald remained conspicuously silent.

"Donald?"

"All right. All right. It's too hot to paddle. Besides, I'm starving. I want a cheeseburger and a vanilla shake."

"A man of perspicacity and vision!" Grog exclaimed. "A true wilderness devotee!"

"You tell the bearded guy he has to take off the dress before I so much as bat an eyeball his direction," Leonore said, joining the fun.

"What's that, madam?"

"You heard me."

"Gladly. Gladly." Grog yanked the tutu down to his ankles and stood buck naked in the sun. The buddies whistled and guffawed. The one with the scaly shoulder tattoos promptly pulled off his shorts and tossed them into the lake.

"I can't believe this," Leonore gasped.

"We advocate nakedness of mind and nakedness of deed!" Grog thundered. His amplified voice rang off the bilious gray lumps of the Clay Hills. "Let's bring reality up from the fine print where it's been languishing and put it back into boldface where it belongs!"

A spasm of nervous laughter rippled through our little flotilla. Here at the end of our memorable adventure, bobbing like a soiled cork, was the irrepressible Grog, *homo Americanus*, beer drinker and bold exhibitionist. It was almost too much for the imagination to bear. The sun continued to hammer the surface of the lake with pitiless fury. I swigged more water and panted in vain for a refreshing draught of air. Grog was a disaster. This lake was a disaster. I never thought I would meet anyone who could make my brother look like an English dandy.

River of Thunder, River of Gold

"Grog, you ought to be locked up and sterilized," Christian groaned.

"What say? What's that?"

"Beer," Billy pleaded through cracked lips. "You got any beer?"

Grog put the bullhorn down and snapped open a Budweiser, showering his face and beard with foam.

"You kids done run out of river, didn't you? And you're feeling a little blue about that, aintcha? Well, hitch up with ole Groggy here and let's get cracking. This sun could fry the brains of a penguin. I don't know about you, but I've had about all the fun I can stand. It's time to git on home."

195

Climbing
Bear Butte

When I told Derrick that I wanted to climb Bear Butte before leaving South Dakota, he laughed and poured a slug of bourbon into a Pepsi glass.

"That's a good idea," he said. "You need to do that. You need to climb right up to the top of that baby."

He took a drink and made a face. It was 5:30 in the afternoon, and we were sitting at the picnic table in the quadrangle of the rangers' quarters. The sun filled the square with a sugary orange glow. Derrick had just gotten off work. The tunic of his uniform was missing two buttons at the point where his stomach bulged out over his belt.

"It's a big hill, so take plenty of water. Best time to climb is late afternoon so you can watch the sunset. It's a different kind of place, so be careful. We got elders from the reservation who go there to pray and fast. It's a high, holy place, man. High *and* holy."

An hour later he wobbled through the door of his unit in the barracks-like complex that walled off one side of the quadrangle. I went next door, pulled all my clothes out of the closet, opened my red riverbag, sat down, and looked at them both. The day after tomorrow I would be on my way home. I either climbed Bear Butte tomorrow or not at all.

Instead of packing I fell asleep. Sometime later I was awakened by blood-curdling screams accompanied by frenzied drumming. Derrick was playing his tribal music tapes. Every evening after his nap he put on a tape and ate an enormous dinner. He claimed the pulsing rhythms and howling cries stimulated his appetite.

"You eaten, man?" he shouted through the thin wall separating the units.

"I'm okay!"

"Don't forget to eat! Keep your strength up! You'll need it for the butte!"

I intended to spend a quiet evening packing and arranging my notes and papers. Around nine Tom Gompers knocked on the door. He was a seasonal ranger who had worked at Badlands National Park since April. He was tall and lanky and wore wire-frame glasses. A tuft of reddish hair dangled from his chin. He looked like a scholarly Quaker.

"A bunch of us are heading to Alf's to have a few beers with Chris and Bev. They're leaving for back east tomorrow. Care to come?"

"Sure. Sounds great."

"Just two beers," Tom cautioned. "Three at the most.

I gotta open the Visitor Center in the morning. Make sure I remember that, will you?"

"You bet. You bet."

Whose idea was it to buy the tequila? By the time the first bottle appeared, we had already consumed enough beer to float a garbage scow across a football field. It wasn't Tom's idea; he was already drunk and fretful about waking up in time to open the V.C. Maybe it was Chris's. That boy was a definite troublemaker. It was certainly his idea to take the bottle up to the top of the hardpacked ridge overlooking the quadrangle.

Around midnight the six of us were sitting on the bare formation passing the second bottle back and forth. The first bottle we had dispatched in the bar. The second went even faster in the open air. We sucked on several lemons, gobbled the pulp, and tossed the rinds into the quadrangle. The sky was clear. The night was moonless. Stars glistened every-where—directly overhead in palpitant clusters, down along the horizon in lustrous spots. The light glowed from the chalkstone cliffs along the White River to the south. The tequila drilled through our brains with the precision of a stiletto. We laughed and cackled and hooted. Out in the washes a pack of coyotes yipped and howled. We mocked their cry, charging the air with quavery yodels.

Then Chris grabbed Bev and shoved her down the hard, bumpy slope. Bev had broken her arm in a horse-back riding accident, and as she tumbled downhill the white cast flashed on and off like a beacon. We waited for her to protest or cry out, but all we heard was an outburst of insane giggling. Chris skidded down after her. We could hear them below, panting and grunting.

Then Tom sprawled on his belly and surfed down the incline, paddling his arms and whooping at the top of his lungs. That seemed like a good idea, so I tried it too. The sun-baked clay peeled the shirt away from my chest. I didn't feel any discomfort, and I reached bottom quicker than I expected. Chris charged back up the slope and grabbed Phil and Shelley and flung them down to the bottom. I didn't approve of his bullying tactics, so I crept up the ridge and jumped him. We grappled awhile, straining and heaving, panting and cursing. I slipped a hand under his thigh and tipped him over the top of the ridge and down the other side. He disappeared into the dark amidst a ripple of foul oaths. Bev reappeared at my side. Her face was torn and cut. Her eyes bulged feverishly. She grabbed the tatters of my shirt and yanked me off-balance. Together in a kind of slow-motion roll, we tumbled down the slope. I landed on top of her. The position was inviting, so I pretended that the wind had been knocked out of me and I couldn't move. She clunked me in the head with her cast. I rolled over into something wet and sticky. Tom was upchucking melodiously into his outstretched fingers.

It was a night of ranger madness. Chris crowed from the top of the ridge and dared anyone to dislodge him. I attempted to crawl back on top of Bev, but she shoved me away. Phil and Shelley got into a terrible fight, and both ended up crying. Tom passed out with his face pressed like a squashed melon against the bare ground. In the distance the coyotes continued to howl. Meteors flashed through the sky like holiday rockets.

The next morning when I examined myself in the mirror I was shocked. My chin and hands were latticed with cuts. Scabby lacerations snaked down my chest and stomach. My shirt was ripped to shreds. Holes gaped in the knees of my trousers.

Hot water from the shower stung the wounds and made me wince. I dried off carefully, blotting myself like an egg. Then I gagged down a cup of sugary coffee and stepped outside. Sunlight drenched the quadrangle. Bev sat alone at the picnic table, hunched over, her neck tucked between her thin shoulders. Her pretty face was as white as a linen napkin.

"I feel like shit," she whispered.

"How's Tom? Have you seen him?"

"Who cares about Tom? I'm supposed to leave today and I can't even stand up without puking."

Her eyes were scored with charcoal bags. She lowered her head onto her arm. "I think I'm going to die."

"I'm off to climb Bear Butte," I announced.

"Good. Have a good time."

"Why don't you come with me?"

"Are you kidding? The wind on my skin makes me sick."

"I'll buy you lunch in Rapid City."

"Go away. Please just go away."

I looked at her small shoulders and trim hips. I had this crazy idea that we could climb Bear Butte together, find a secluded spot near the summit, take off our clothes, and make a prayer to the spirits.

I retreated disconsolately over the dry grass. A shoe lay at the edge of the quadrangle with the laces missing. Closeby coiled the length of a frayed black belt. A light wind skipped over the brown weeds. Derrick ambled up the walk from the parking lot dressed in ranger green and a peaked cap. His swarthy face was puffy, the cheeks intagliated with tiny pockmarks. "What the hell you guys do last night?" he said.

"We had a little party."

"It sounded like a bunch of cats fucking in an out-house. I never heard such a racket."

"We had a fun time."

"Indians don't sound like that, man, when they get drunk. They just boil in their own sweat."

"We need to take lessons from you guys, I guess."

"You're all crippled up. Chris, he looks like a badger ate his face. I ain't seen Tom. He still alive, you think?"

"I dunno. He passed out and we had to put him to bed. I don't think he got up in time to open the V.C."

"You still planning to climb Bear Butte?"

"I got to. I go home tomorrow."

"Shit, man, you're in no shape to do that."

"I'll make it okay."

"I don't mean that. I mean in your head. Your head ain't right, man. It's full of booze."

I found my car where I'd parked it half on the grass and half on the asphalt. The engine kicked over; I drove past the Visitor Center then up the bleak face of the Badlands Wall. The view from the top—a pan-oramic sweep of eroded tables and orphaned buttes—was impressive. For sheer desolation there are few spectacles to match it. Along a strip of land forty miles wide by one hundred miles long, situated between the Cheyenne and White rivers, the Badlands extends in a blistered ribbon. Slashed by pelting rain, baked by savage heat, peeled by cutting winds, the land is almost totally denuded of vegetation. Preserved in the colorful strata of clay deposits are the fossilized remains of prehistoric animals, including diminutive three-toed deer and the bulky titanotheres, a rhino-like creature with a spatulate horn. In the old days the Indians gave the region a wide berth. *Mako Sica,* they called it, the place of malevolent spirits. Rattlesnakes invested the ravines and gullies. The grass was thin *Climbing* and patchy; few buffalo ventured into the area. There *Bear* was little wood with which to build winter quarters or *Butte* even light a fire. A type of wolf, lean and surly, colored a milky gray like the hard-baked clay, prowled for rabbits and mice. Early French explorers named the place *mauvais terres*. George Armstrong Custer described it as "a part of hell with the fires burned out."

One afternoon Tom Gompers and I crawled up the face of the Badlands Wall, slithering through ruts and crevices, twisting through tube-like holes which the rain had cored out of the soil. When we reached the top after a climb of a hundred feet or more, squeezing through passageways tunneled out like prairie-dog holes, we were puffing and blowing. We staggered out into the sunlight and gazed to the south past sculpted buttes and flat-topped tables toward the White River and the Pine Ridge Reservation. "It gets me every time," Tom confessed. "I love to work my way up through the earth like that. It's like one of those Indian stories about the creation of the world. It's like evolving into a new state of being."

I stopped at a Denny's on the outskirts of Rapid City and wolfed down a cheese omelette and a plate of cottage fries. The hangover had infected the major joints of my body. I moved like a robot on rusty hinges. My mouth felt as if a family of moles had soiled it with their droppings. A scrawny waitress with curly brown hair kept refilling my coffee cup.

"You look like you could use a lot of this," she said.

"What I really need is a blood transfusion," I sighed.

"We don't do those, but I'd be happy to serve you some dessert."

The greasy lunch added to my edginess. I felt jittery

and disconnected, as if someone had crept into my room last night and pieced together the parts of my shattered nervous system while wearing a blindfold and mittens.

Puffy clouds ladened with moisture were already forming over the Black Hills behind Rapid City. The sight stirred my memory. In July, accompanied by an official from the Oglala Parks and Recreation Department, I had bumped in a Ford Bronco along a dirt track across Cuny Table, in the remote south unit of the park. With us was a tribal elder named Henry Shoots-the-Bear. Henry was an American Indian Movement activist; during the turbulent days of the 1970s he'd been in the thick of the conflict on the reservation between Indian dissidents and Bureau of Indian Affairs authorities. He was an attractive, soft-spoken, leathery-faced man in his mid-sixties. At the north rim of Cuny Table we got out of the Bronco and peered across the narrow isthmus of land leading to Stronghold Table.

Stronghold Table holds a special place in the hearts of the Oglala Sioux. It was here that the Ghost Dancers assembled in the fall of 1890, far away from the meddlesome eyes of white authorities. Standing there with Henry, I could easily understand why Stronghold Table had been selected as the dancers' retreat. The sides dropped hundreds of feet to a desolate plain. The neck of land connecting Cuny Table with Stronghold was no wider than a drawbridge across the moat of a medieval castle. According to Henry there were two springs on Stronghold in 1890. The dancers set up their tipis in a traditional circle, with an opening to the east and the horses corraled inside. Criers went from dwelling to dwelling calling out instructions and information. With the buffalo virtually exterminated, the dancers brought their own cattle, which ranged freely over the grassy surface. A line of rifle pits was dug across Cuny Table to protect the approaches to Climbing Stronghold. From the rim, sentinels could see long *Bear* distances across the badlands. Secluded on their re- *Butte* mote eyrie, the dancers were free to pursue their vision of a resurrected world where buffalo were abundant, the dead were restored to life, and the hated *wasicu* was still living in European ghettos.

"We can't let you go over there," Henry said. "It's a special site for us."

"That's all right. I understand."

Instead we walked through rippling waist-high grass to a low mound. The parks and recreation official stayed behind in the vehicle, smoking a cigarette. To the west, seventy miles away, the outline of the Black Hills was neatly etched against the horizon. The rugged slopes were draped with pine forests, which gave them a dark, brooding complexion.

Henry and I stood quietly in the sweet morning air. The cheery song of a meadowlark crinkled against our ears. Heat waves shimmered off Cuny Table, distorting the profile of the distant hills. A marsh hawk, a bold white spot marking its rump, swooped back and forth over the rim.

"I will tell you a story about Crazy Horse," Henry began in a soft voice that I had to strain to hear. "You know there are always two versions of history, the Indian and the white. One is written down and the other is passed by word of mouth from generation to generation. They don't always sound the same, but anyone who wants to know the truth must be aware of both."

I folded my arms across my chest. There was something dignified and appealing about this man. His face was handsome and grave, with prominent cheekbones under his narrow eyes. A broadbrim hat rested squarely on the crown of his well-formed skull.

"Before the Battle of Little Big Horn, Crazy Horse

sent a message to your General Custer. '*Wasicu*,' it said, 'a struggle will soon take place between my people and yours. In this struggle you will die and all of your people. You are a brave man, but foolish. You have the courage of a buffalo, but not the intelligence. At the end of this battle, *wasicu*, I will cut open your chest and eat your heart. Your death will make me strong, and I will live to kill many more of your people."

I reached the parking lot at Bear Butte State Park around one o'clock. I'd forgotten to bring a canteen and a hat. The lower reaches of the butte were drenched in blazing light. The trail was wide and well-marked. It wound up the steep sides in a series of tight switchbacks. The summit was over a thousand feet high, a reasonable climb.

Bear Butte pokes up by itself off the plains, a lonely monolith, six miles northeast of the Black Hills. Geologically the butte is a laccolith, or a volcano that never erupted. "That's what gives it its power," Derrick explained to me. "It's got all this force pent up inside that's never been released. Medicine people like to tap into that."

Magma welling up from the crust of the earth had frothed and lathered in a fit of angry waves before finally settling and hardening into basaltic slabs. But it never blew its top. If it had, the profile would be marked by a major crater. Near the summit, wind and rain have worn the soil off the rock, revealing the igneous core. Bear Butte is a geologist's dream; the salient features are easy to observe. Like a buffalo skull bleaching on the hard ground or a sundancer dangling from a cottonwood pole, it stands exposed for all the world to see.

206

From the highway the butte resembles the outline of *Climbing* a sleeping bear. Bears have long been associated with *Bear* it. George Custer shot a grizzly near the site during *Butte* his 1874 Black Hills expedition in search of gold. He then had the misfortune to have himself and the animal photographed with the butte clearly visible in the background. His Arikara scouts warned him that he was courting bad medicine. Two years later Crazy Horse ate his heart.

The butte abounds in legends. The Lakota tell a story about a vicious battle between a bear and a dinosaur that lasted for days. So fiercely did the animals fight that rivers of blood drenched the earth. Finally the dinosaur wounded the bear so terribly he slumped onto his side. As he groaned in agony the ground erupted and darkness descended like a pall. Volcanoes fumed and roared, ash and fire spewed into the sky. Then the chaos ceased; the darkness melted away and the air became sparkling and clear. Where the dying bear had lain a huge hill now loomed. Under the steep sides, plainly visible, rested the figure of the slain bear.

I was trembling as I started up the trail; my knees were weak and unsteady. The sun beat down against my hatless head. Yucca and prickly pear pronged out of the flaky soil. In the gullies and ravines grew dense thickets of sumac, berry vines, and Virginia creeper. The view widened as I climbed higher. Magnificent grasslands unfolded to the north and east; to the southwest lurked the gloomy bulk of the Black Hills. Clouds thickened over the rounded summits in curvaceous tiers.

The switchbacks were steep. I took my time, pausing to enjoy the view, to catch my breath, to sniff the scaly orange bark of a ponderosa. Down a side path, dangling from low-hanging branches, were patches of multi-colored cloth. I stopped to look at them. A moment or two elapsed before my eyes detected, through a screen of pine needles, the head, chest, and shoulders of a burly man. My heart gave a little flutter. The man's back was partially turned to the main trail. He was peering intently into a shadowy cleft of junipers that bristled between two rock outcroppings. His hair was long and knotted into a queue. His skull was bound in a red bandana. He didn't appear to be aware of my presence. The cloth patches stirred sluggishly in the dry breeze that luffed through the trees. The patches signaled the cardinal directions of a complex spiritual compass; that much I knew. To what degree the symbols were meaningful to the man, I had no way of knowing. I felt like an intruder, and I tried to step lightly. When I looked back again the man was nowhere to be seen.

On up I trudged. My leg muscles jerked at odd moments as if sparked by an electric charge. From a scree of rocks cobbling the foot of a talus slope a snake suddenly appeared, curling over the pebbles carpeting the trail. I started back then caught myself and leaned forward, one hand on my hip, attentive and alert. The snake was two feet long. Black spots dappled its iridescent back. It didn't flare up or hiss at my presence. It slithered across the trail and disappeared into the bush.

By the time I reached the summit an hour later I was dripping with sweat. The cuts on my chest and hands stung from the tang of the salt. Other than the man between the trees, I'd seen no one on the trail. It was as if I had the mountain to myself, though I knew that wasn't the case. I had passed too many prayer sites, with bright flags fluttering from the trees. Of all the elevated power spots dotting the Great Plains, Bear

Butte is arguably the most celebrated. Red Cloud, *Climbing* Crazy Horse, and Sitting Bull all sought guidance and *Bear* consolation here. Visions had been invoked and an- *Butte* cestors importuned. It was here that Wakan Tanka vis-ited Crazy Horse's father and instructed him to pass on his name to his illustrious son. It was here that Sweet Medicine, sacred leader of the Cheyennes, gave his people their first religious artifacts.

The summit was disappointing. Some genius in the South Dakota State Park System had erected a wooden platform with a railing across the rocky crown. The platform was silly and intrusive; holy sites aren't supposed to be accessible to everyone. It converted the summit into an observation post rather than a place of meditation and prayer. It encouraged people to think that once they reached the top all they had to do was admire the view, snap a few photos, and trot back down.

I climbed the final steps and clomped across the boards. To the southwest rose the moody slopes of the Black Hills. Additional clouds, grumbly with rain, had gathered over the peaks. But here at the top of Bear Butte the sun beamed down. I squinted into the glare. Two flies careened around my head banging my cheeks and forehead. Sentinel flies, no doubt, assigned by the gods to challenge anyone who made it this far. *Who are you? What are you doing here?* they seemed to say through their maniacal buzzing.

The flies banged against my neck and shoulders. I swatted at them, but they wouldn't go away. I had encountered their kind before, especially at oases in the Southern California deserts. The flies monitor not only the supply of water there, but the approaches to it. They remind us that in arid landscapes water is more precious than gold. It is the source of life, never to be wasted or soiled. And just in case you have forgotten how to behave, here are a few reminders. Bzzz! Rrrpt! Whfft! A smack or two against the side of the face reinforces the point.

I finally took refuge under the platform. It was cool there; the shadows were slotted with bands of light from the cracks between the planks. The flies didn't follow. I sighed and drew my knees up under my chin. I felt fatigued and listless. The climb had siphoned the energy from my body. Uneasiness gnawed at my bowels. The research I had done for my little book on the Oglala Sioux—the texts I had read, the people I had interviewed, the ceremonies I had attended— what did it all mean? I felt estranged from my subject like a man in a pin-striped suit picking his way through a crowd of hooded vendors in a Moroccan souk. I felt incapable of writing anything authentic or insightful about the Oglala and their culture. I could list the important details, string them together into a readable narrative, which is what the Park Service had hired me to do. But to write something with depth and feeling, sensitivity and perception, from a point of view that included both factual observation and thoughtful synthesis, seemed beyond my capabilities. The subject was too complex, my experience too limited.

Something else bothered me, too. As long as I was under the platform, out of reach of the flies, I felt I ought to confess it. I was fearful that all this research and investigation had turned me into a voyeur. An anthropological voyeur, the sort that feasts off the carcasses of other cultures. What right-thinking person could possibly not be attracted to certain aspects of Native American life? The history, the religion, the customs pointed to the possibility of a rich and meaningful life. However, in the process, I had filched a few of their possessions. Nothing concrete or monetary, no artifacts or *objets d'art*, just a few stories and legends. I had practiced a kind of theft, certainly more

210

subtle than burning villages and stealing land, but an act of exploitation nonetheless. I had embraced the Oglala Sioux with the earnestness of my good intentions (or perhaps the pathology of my own spiritual malaise), and I wondered if the embrace wasn't every bit as suffocating in its own way as the guardposts that once ringed the reservations, or the beer and whiskey bars that ring them now.

I must have fallen asleep for a few minutes. When I opened my eyes I didn't know where I was. The space under the platform was grilled with shadows; I felt like a POW in a bamboo cage. Out through the opening between the rocky summit and the platform I could see stormclouds stacking up over the Black Hills. I shook my head and pinched my cheeks. In addition to everything else it looked as if I might get rained on.

Something whacked against my cheek with a stinging wallop. The flies had found me down here in the shadows. They buzzed my head and shoulders with ravenous fury. It sounded as if they wanted to eat me alive. Never before had I encountered such testy flies. The reek of stale booze must have incited them. *What are you doing here?* they demanded. *What right do you have to be here?*

And indeed, at that moment, I didn't feel as if I had much right. My nerves were frazzled. My energy had dwindled. Whatever it was that I had toiled up these slopes to find simply was not forthcoming. Bear Butte's secrets were safe from my inquiring eyes. Perhaps at another time I might feel more connected to the place. As for now the flies were correct; I was an interloper, an outlander. Better that I sober up before attempting the climb again.

I cursed and swatted wildly at the varmints. They

buzzed gleefully out of reach. Dazed, my head pounding, I crawled out from under the platform and stood up. The dark clouds over the Black Hills were advancing in solemn dreadnoughts toward Bear Butte. I stumbled down the trail. Within minutes the temperature dropped as the edge of the storm advanced across the prairie. Thunder rumbled ominously. Lightning crackled against the lower slopes. The reek of ozone drifted between the trees. The leaves and needles, the plants, the blades of grass poking up through the trail grew intensely quiet. The storm rolled up the west face of the butte like an artillery barrage. I had barely taken cover under a piñon tree when it broke with savage fury. Rain slanted down in drenching sheets that seeped through the boughs, soaking my head and shoulders. Lightning stunned the air with deafening bolts. The ground shook and trembled. Rivulets of muddy water fanned out from the trail. A black stinkbug, crawling past the heel of my boot, suddenly stood on its head and elevated its haunches. Not a bad idea, I thought, as I buried my face in my arms and curled my body into a fetal coil.

The storm had shaken it out of me, and for the first time that day I felt settled and relaxed. It was as if the angry force of the wind and rain had pelted me with sufficient vigor to soothe my skittish nerves. Thoroughly soaked, my boots squishing, I descended the rest of the way with the solemn pomp of a funeral cortege. The trail was littered with twigs and branches. The sparse vegetation on the lower slopes had the bedraggled look of wet dog hair. The storm had poured forth its wrath and passed on; from the parking lot I watched the raft of surly clouds fume and rumble over the flatlands.

I took route 44, a state road that rambles southeast of Rapid City. I'd had enough of interstates and park- ing lots and wooden platforms. Route 44 rises and falls over undulating ridges divided by gravelly washes and dotted with grazing cattle. Between Caputa and Farm- ingdale the evening sun broke through the clouds, gild- ing the damp grass. Pearly drops glistened from the trees like Christmas ornaments.

The smell of rain on the asphalt, slick and clean, mingled with the fragrant scent of wet sage that seeped in through the window. I inhaled and growled hun- grily. There was one can of soup left in the kitchen of my unit. Derrick might ask me to eat with them. His wife, a Northern Cheyenne woman, was a gifted cook, and she was generous about setting an extra plate at their table.

The car dipped toward the Cheyenne River. Over the next rise, a few miles to the east, the land buckled and warped into the lunar desolation of the Badlands. There on the edge, like an ugly toad, squatted the mis- named town of Scenic, home of the Longhorn Bar, one of the genuinely *bad* Western saloons. A ramshackled building, built of warped clapboards, it sported a cage by the front door with a sign that read, in faded Lakota, "Don't Feed the Drunken Indian." Inside was a long bar and round tables with sawdust littering the floor. The ceiling was scored with cattle brands and bullet holes. The Indians drank at the back tables, the whites at the bar. Occasionally there were fights, but Crocker, the man who ran the place—a paunchy man with a belt-length white beard—maintained order and peace. He kept a gun and a hickory club within easy reach. He liked to brag that he ran a family place. In- dian children played with empty beer bottles in the sawdust while their parents drank quietly at the tables.

Traffic on Route 44 was moderate. I cruised along at fifty miles per hour thinking about a hot shower and sleep. The shadows rising out of the gullies and ravines contrasted boldly with the sunny expanse of short grass where cattle wandered and meadowlarks trilled. Down the road in front of the bridge I spotted two figures walking my direction along the shoulder. I let up on the accelerator. By the time the car drew abreast of them, it was traveling at forty miles per hour. They were an Indian man and woman, evidently hoofing from the reservation to Rapid City. They were young, dressed in tight jeans and blousy shirts. The man wore cowboy boots, not exactly the best hiking gear, though he didn't appear to be in discomfort. The woman wore Nikes. She walked with a steady, shuffling gait, several yards behind the man. A ballcap pulled down over her face cast a shadow to her chin. Glossy hair rippled out from under the cap like a pennant.

But what caught my attention—what riveted it— was the baby the man cradled in the crook of his arm. The light from the setting sun beamed over the rounded humps of the Black Hills, illumining the wet road, the trees, the sparkling grasslands, illumining the baby's copper cheeks and howling mouth. The wind clawed at the man and woman, stiffening their features and filling their clothes like sails. And then the car rolled past. I wanted to turn around and go back and look at them again, but I didn't. I couldn't. They weren't specimens in a curio shop, and I had some sensitivity to their privacy as human beings.

The car reached the bridge. The Cheyenne River gushed with the runoff from the downpour. The banks were fringed with green weeds that gave off a slick chlorophyll smell. As the car chugged up the other side, I looked back again. Backlit by the fading sun, the Black Hills glowed like a lump of coal. Before passing over the crest I saw something that made me cry out loud. The woman continued to plod forward, head down, her arms barely swinging at her sides. The man, *Climbing* out front, clutching the infant between his hands, sud- *Bear* denly held it up—as high as his long arms would *Butte* reach; the fringes of the buckskin pouch flapping wildly in the wind—to catch the last rays of sunlight slanting over the ancient humps of the hills.

In Animals
We Find Ourselves

The sea was uneasy that afternoon as we started out in the small boat. The wind had shifted to the northwest, kicking up frothy whitecaps that slopped over the sides of the nine-foot skiff as it skimmed from crest to crest. We were bundled up to the eyeballs in warm clothing, but that didn't prevent the frigid air from knifing to our bones. We sat like frozen puppets on the hard-planked seats, clinging with stiff fingers to any loop or handle we could find as the boat lurched up and down.

There were three of us—Ray Malone, Dan Streeter, and myself. Malone was a bearded, thickset man in his mid-thirties, an official from the Alaska Department of Fish and Game. Over several layers of warm clothing he wore a fluorescent orange Mercury survival suit. He looked like any other researcher you might encounter in the Bering Sea except for one detail: slung across his back was a polished, well-oiled .222 rifle with a telescopic lens.

Dan Streeter sat in the stern, with one big hand curled around the throttle of the twenty-five horsepower engine. Dan was in his mid-twenties—tall, stout, attractive, with curly brown hair and cat-green eyes. He was studying for a PhD in geology at Yale. From the deck of the *Alpha Helix*, the 130-foot research vessel that had carried us into the eastern Bering Sea, he could look at the ice-bound mountains of the Alaskan Peninsula and weave a wonderful story of their origins. This afternoon his face bore a troubled expression; the smile that habitually played around the corners of his wide mouth was compressed into a solemn line.

Our destination was Strogonoff Point, a bare, featureless spit jutting out from the Alaskan Peninsula. The spit loomed out of the dreary sea in a low, blurry rise some two miles east of the spot where the *Alpha Helix* had dropped her anchor that morning. The volcanic sand clinging to the sloping berm was only slightly darker than the murky waves on which we pitched and tossed. It was a little like racing toward a mirage that seemed perpetually on the brink of disappearing. The icy mountains protruding from the peninsula's backbone appeared totally unrelated to the illusion of the spit, like a distant backdrop deftly sketched in to accentuate the latitudinal sweep of space.

When we were still some ways from shore, Malone, squatting next to me on the center seat, popped open the white lid of an ice chest and pulled out a .357 Magnum revolver. As best he could in the bobbing craft, he slipped five ugly, snub-nosed shells into the chamber, slid the revolver back into the holster, and returned the holster to the chest. Stenciled across the grainy red plastic back of the chest in faded letters was "MALONE—ALASKA DEP'T OF FISH & GAME." This particular afternoon the chest was filled not with beer and sandwiches but with glass tubes, syringes, sharp knives, Hefty garbage bags, twist-top waterproof sacks, a Minolta camera, and scores of plastic tags. "If a grizzly comes sniffing around while we're on shore, you might wave the revolver at him," Malone shouted to Dan. "Maybe he might get the message. Maybe not."

Dan nodded bravely. I nodded, too, and got set to jump out of the skiff with Malone. It was early afternoon, and a vigorous tide swirled against the point. Where the waves swept up the face of the gritty swash, a damp sheet remained imprinted upon the porous sand. As the boat heaved through a final eruption of surf, I spotted a slew of tiny, quartz-like pebbles tumbling down the slope. The bow crunched the sand. We leaped over the sides and slogged up the berm in our bulky clothes. A harsh wind sliced against our faces, bringing tears to my eyes. Malone took advantage of the elevation to examine the terrain. That morning, while scanning the beach from the bridge of the *Alpha Helix*, the first mate had spotted a grizzly prowling along the spit.

As we moved along the berm, parallel with the water, I kept turning around and looking over my shoulder. The berm was tufted with clumps of coarse grass. Buoys, glass bottles, lengths of rope, net fragments formed a scraggly line at the highwater mark. There wasn't a scrap of cover anywhere that could conceal a creature the size of a grizzly, much less anything smaller. The spit was narrow, maybe fifty yards wide. A quarter-mile to the north the tip thinned to a soggy

219

trace before sliding underwater. The spit formed a protective barrier, walling off a placid lagoon from the charging surf. Miles to the east, their jagged peaks mantled with snow, rose a phalanx of stolid mountains.

The sand was marked with seal tracks, evidence that the animals had recently hauled out on the beach. Malone was perplexed by the fact that so many had assembled in one spot within feasting range of the grizzlies. "Seals usually haul out on offshore islands where the bears can't reach them," he explained.

He pulled the .222 rifle off his shoulder and sighted through the telescopic lens. The seals were in the water a few yards offshore, their dark heads bobbing in the high chop like bits of burnt cork.

I could feel Malone's frustration. We had to maneuver within range. "We can't get to them from here!" he hollered over the bite of the wind. "Let's get back to the boat!"

But not all the animals had returned to the water. A baby seal, three or four days old, pawed the sand behind a clump of tundra that had washed up on shore. The pup was three feet long with a tubular body piebald with brown and gray spots. He barked pathetically and swung his head back and forth.

"Looks like he got separated from his mother in the last haul-out," Malone observed. "She's probably out there, looking for him."

"What if she can't find him?"

"He'll most likely die. He hasn't been weaned yet. Either that or a grizzly will get him."

I went down on one knee. The pup had no teeth, but that didn't prevent him from nipping at my gloved hand as I stroked his head. He barked again with a honking burp and wrenched his head from side to side.

"Is there some way we can help?" I said.

"We can try and get him back into the water. His mother might find him then."

The wind ripped against our faces. Before the sea became impossible to navigate, Malone wanted to take advantage of the plentiful seals in view offshore. A classic conflict was building between scientific necessity and humanitarian ardor. I voiced my concern to Malone.

"We can have both!" he boomed in my ear. "But we've got to move fast!"

Back in the skiff, with Dan at the throttle, we churned along the shore looking for seals. A dozen heads popped out of the water, their round eyes regarding us quizzically. Malone stood in the bow, his feet braced firmly apart. With so many targets he could be selective. The water heaved and swelled. It was like being in an arena where everyone, hunter and prey alike, glided around on roller skates.

I squatted mid-skiff, clutching the harpoon and plastic buoy. Malone zeroed in on a whiskered face a few yards off the starboard bow. This moment was always the worst. I mumbled an inaudible plea. "Miss, Malone. Miss, goddammit." Though I knew he wouldn't. He was a crack shot. And he needed the seal. The tension twisted into a spiky knot inside my chest.

The report, flat and metallic, slammed across the water. "Go!" Malone shouted. Dan cranked the throttle, and the skiff lurched toward a bright stain slicking the waves. Malone handed me the rifle; I passed him the harpoon. Dead seals sink fast, and we had already lost several by not reaching them in time. The boat slalomed alongside the floating carcass. Dan cut the power. Malone braced one knee against the starboard gunwhale, and wheeling both arms high overhead, plunged the harpoon with a cutting smack deep into the hide. I tossed over the buoy. If the seal sank, we had it marked.

I handed the rifle back to Dan, plunged both hands into frigid water, and slowly and gingerly pulled the

221

carcass toward the boat. Seal blood stained the dull sea a livid red. Grasping the animal by the front flippers, Malone and I turned it around. Then, taking firm hold of the rear flippers, we tugged and pulled the hind quarters over the gunwhale. Blood fountained in a tiny arc from a hole in the animal's head. The spectacle against the monochromatic backdrop of the Alaskan Peninsula made me swallow hard. In the tropics it might go unnoticed, but here in this drab wilderness it impressed itself indelibly upon my consciousness.

I lashed the seal to the thwart and wrapped a plastic tag around the rear flipper. Malone pulled the spent cartridge out of the rifle and bolted a fresh one into the breech. He nodded at Dan, who cranked the throttle. Slowly, stealthily, we circled through the restless waves. The sea was broken into tilted slabs that sloshed and jostled one another. At the sound of the gun the other seals had disappeared as if wiped from a slate. Now, one by one, prompted by curiosity or lack of air, they popped back into view. Malone planted his feet again and brought the rifle to his shoulder. The boat tipped and he staggered forward, catching himself with one hand. I slid over and wrapped my arms around his ankles. One time I had let my brother use my shoulder as a mount from which to take aim at a rabbit nibbling in the grass. Fortunately, he missed. Malone didn't. The explosion rang across the water with the clamor of steel blocks crashing together. Within an hour we had three more. Weighed down by nearly a thousand pounds of specimens, the boat nudged through the sea.

I had never done work like this before. Malone was conducting the first scientific collection of harbor seals in the eastern Bering Sea. The purpose of the work was to provide a data base from which to determine the overall state of health of harbor seals in the region. "In a few years this coastline is going to be thrown open to oil exploration, and you know what that means," he told us after our first day. "Spills, blow-outs, tanker collisions, the whole ecological nightmare. We need to know everything we can about harbor seals. One way is to examine their scat, but since they do it in the water, that's impractical. The other is what we're doing. It's not easy, but it offers the best results. Researchers at the University of Alaska in Fairbanks will analyze the blood and tissue samples for evidence of toxic poisons and trace minerals. The stomach contents will be examined, and the reproductive organs. All this should give us a fairly solid foundation from which to make any future assessments."

After winching the carcasses onto the fantail of the *Alpha Helix*, I helped Malone cut open the bodies and remove the organs. Dan usually chose this moment to disappear into the galley for a cup of coffee. I stayed with Malone, out of curiosity at first, and then for more complex reasons. As the days passed, I developed an identification with the animal that carried far beyond mere scientific inquiry. Not only did the sight of the seal's blood remind me of our consanguinity, but the abdomen of an adult harbor seal is approximately the size of an adult human male's. Each time I reached into the tangled viscera, I felt as if I were reaching for something deep inside myself. As I picked through the sticky folds of the seal's heart collecting worms, I felt my own heart sputter and knock.

The gulls that ranged over the fantail as we bent to our work eyed as hungrily. Whenever I found myself becoming overwrought with burdensome thoughts, I tried to keep in mind what the seals meant to them. A bit of food. Protein to absorb. Fecal matter to deposit. Purely utilitarian concerns. Unfortunately the demands of scientific collecting left them little to en- joy. By the time we peeled off the seal's hide, removed the organs, cut off the head, and coiled the intestines into a plastic sack, there wasn't much to give back to the sea. The gulls screamed in protest whenever we rolled a stripped and plucked cadaver over the rail and dropped it into the waves.

Slowly the tally of specimens increased. Ideally, Malone wanted between twenty and twenty-five to take back to his researchers. Sometimes, especially when the weather closed in, we came back empty- handed. But we went out nearly every day, in fair weather or foul. And as the days passed, our care and attention to the details of the job increased. We weighed the seals and taped their length. We mea- sured the width of their flippers and the thickness of their pelts. We drew blood from their spinal arteries. Gradually the data accumulated. Gradually our knowl- edge enlarged. Gradually our affection intensified. These simple details, recorded in a dog-eared yellow notebook with careful fidelity, began to assume the substance of a litany. When Malone brought an organ out of an open body for me to tag and deposit in a plastic sack, he did so in a thoughtful and deliberate manner. The process of excoriation was revelatory, both in regard to the seal's anatomy and my own feel- ings. By his steady example, Malone demonstrated the intrinsic value of work honorably performed, how it can lend dignity and shape to the most difficult task. Under his tutelage a revelation slowly stole over me. The physical body contains functional properties, the proper acknowledgment of which can transform them into a fresh order of sacraments. Blood is a transfigur- ing element. It calls forth the deepest emotional com- mitment a person is capable of.

But there were moments when the ritualization

224

failed to counteract the brutal truth of what we were doing. One afternoon in the wave-tossed surf off Ugashik Bay we killed a pregnant female. We knew there was something extra to her weight when, puffing and straining, we hauled her into the skiff. We had just finished pulling her over the gunwhale, and I was reaching out to secure her with a rope, when a spasm rippled the length of her body, and she died.

I stared at the top of her sleek head in shock and consternation. Then, tremulous with sorrow, I lowered my face and pressed my cheek against her cold hide.

Later, on the fantail, Malone levered the tip of the big knife gingerly through the adbominal cortex. The outline of a lifeless pup was visible through the ghostly sheath of the amniotic sack. I felt my stomach rush up through my throat. Another cut and the fetus, stumpy and compact, slid into my hands. Breath escaped from my lips in an audible gasp. The pup was two feet long and weighed around fifteen pounds. Dark freckles dotted the smooth greenish-gray hide. The eyes were sealed, the mouth pasted back in a taut grimace. The sides of the pointed snout were plastered with bristly whiskers.

Malone winced and brought the hand with the knife up to his face as if to block out the sight. "Oh Lord," he groaned. "This is hard. This is so hard sometimes."

Inside the crowded skiff there was little room to move. An agitated sea broke repeatedly over the sides. The outboard engine strained against the load. I got busy bailing. Dan was preoccupied with the engine. Malone drew samples from the spinal arteries of the latest specimens. A vigorous wind pummeled our backs and shoulders. The weather was turning sour. This evening we would probably be in for a blow. The seals in the water didn't seem to mind. As if excited by the approaching storm, they thrust their heads up through the waves.

With an obliging shove from an incoming wave, the skiff slithered against the sand and quartz pebbles speckling the shoreline of the point. "You guys check on the little fellow while I secure things here," Malone called. "It's a long ride out to the *Alpha*. We'd better have things fastened down before we start."

Dan shut off the engine and tilted the prop out of the water. Then he eased his big body over the side. His attractive face was moody and troubled. He hadn't said much all afternoon. There was a heaviness to his presence, a solemnity, that seemed out of keeping with his normally jovial character.

We found the pup flailing the sand with his small flippers behind the same clump of loose tundra. He barked and croaked and made a feeble attempt to propel himself forward. Finally he gave up and lowered his nose to the sand. A fine rain pelted our cheeks. Dan knelt down and placed his hand on the pup's head. "Malone's right," he growled. "He's a goner if we leave him here. We gotta get him in the water."

Sure, I thought, and then what? No matter what we did the pup didn't stand much of a chance. The irony was withering. To satisfy the interests of science we had just killed four seals. Now we were excited about the fate of a single pup. And no matter what solution we devised, the pup would most likely die within twenty-four hours of starvation, of drowning, or between the teeth of a grizzly.

I stared at Dan. Water dribbled off the peaked bill of his cap. His dark eyebrows were bunched together in a bushy line. "Hell, I don't know," he snarled. "I'm a rock man. I don't know how to take care of little guys like

226

this. But we just can't stand here like a couple of turnips."

The pup squealed when I picked him up. I tightened my grip around his squirming body, carried him down to the beach, and lowered him into the surf. The first wave bowled him over; the second knocked him back up on his flippers. He seemed unfamiliar with the water and ill at ease. He honked and tried to lumber up the sand out of reach of the cold waves.

"Damn," said Dan. "He won't go in alone. He doesn't know how."

It was a curious moment. I felt as if I were dangling at the end of a long, frayed string. A raft of contrary emotions charged through me.

Without a word Dan took off toward the tip of the barrier spit a quarter-mile away, his rubber boots thunking against the damp volcanic sand. I watched him go without protest and sat down beside the pup. Pulling off my glove, I smoothed two fingers over the bony knob of his skull. The pup grunted hollowly. The hair on his narrow head was thin and warm. The shape of the skull was familiarly dog-like, but my stroking failed to bring him relief. Instead he barked in urgent yaps and swung his blunt, baby-whiskered face back and forth on the muscular stub of his neck.

Something clutched at my chest. I was filled with a memory of myself as a child. It was during the war, the early 1940s. My mother had been diagnosed with what was thought to be terminal cancer. Twice a week she went for treatments at a clinic in a suburb of Washington, D.C., where we lived. Unable to obtain a babysitter for my brother and me, she took us along and left us in the car, with the doors locked and our faces pressed against the glass. I don't know if we cried when she left or tried to comfort one another, or what. I only remember the distinct and detailed image of her disappearing behind a row of clipped hedges, then magically reappearing on a stoop in front of a wooden door with a heavy knocker that she grasped with both hands. The door swung open revealing a woman in a white uniform who smiled and stepped aside to let her enter. The door closed, and she disappeared again, forever, it seemed. The wrench of parting created a shock the effects of which I still feel today. And yet she always emerged, she always returned to the car, albeit weak and a bit unsteady; she always unlocked the door and slid behind the wheel and flashed us a sweet, ambiguous smile. She always managed to drive us home. How to explain this? She didn't die; she lived for a number of years. So many people have gone through much worse things. And yet the pang at being left behind under those circumstances has haunted me as much as any single event in my life; and now on this treeless, wind-scoured strip of Alaskan coast, it filled my chest again. I was bonded to the little seal by more than blood. I wanted to cry but I had too much to do. Thank God I had too much to do.

Dan trotted back on the double from the far end of the spit. His face was bright and hopeful. "There're three baby seals down there!" he shouted. "They all look as if they've been abandoned! There's a sea lion too, but I chased him away!"

The sea lion wasn't encouraging. Males have been known to devour infant seals. But we had no choice. I gathered the pup in my arms and stumbled after Dan. The seal groaned and wiggled. He only weighed about twenty pounds, but he was difficult to handle. I clutched him tightly and puffed along, trying to keep pace with Dan's longer strides. "You want me to carry him?" he said.

"I got him! I got him!"

It was like hefting a bag of liquid. With each step

228

the pup seemed to swell and bulge. I needed another arm to hold him securely.

Three pups with splotchy, light-colored coats clung to the edge of the spit. The sea lion had vanished. An outgoing tide boiled over the submerged prow of the tip, creating a distinct eddy line. Water was emptying out of Strogonoff Lagoon at a rapid clip; in an hour or two long stretches of the sheltered bay would be exposed to the gulls and grizzlies. Clearly visible a few yards offshore were a dozen harbor seals, their smooth heads dipping and gliding in the frothy surf. I put the pup down next to the others. The closest pup, probably obeying some territorial instinct, reached out and smacked the newcomer in the face with a front flipper.

"Hey!" I yelled. "Cut that out!"

I stepped back next to Dan. We fidgeted helplessly like a pair of anxious parents. The other seals poked and nudged our guy in an unfriendly manner. They looked a little bigger, a little older. Even with their example, I wondered if he could swim.

"Now what?"

"Who knows?" Dan bellowed. "Let's see what happens!"

Something must have sounded a signal. One by one the seals waddled off the spit and disappeared into the surf. Our guy hesitated, glanced at the water, then back at us. "Go! Go!" we cried. "Get into the water! The water!"

Slowly he staggered into the waves and ducked out of sight. A moment later he reappeared, several yards out. He poked his head up, looked back, then slipped under the churning tide.

Dan and I were ecstatic. We hooted wildly and danced up and down and clapped one another on the back. Relieved and delighted, we trudged back along the beach through a buffeting wind to help Malone carry his precious cargo out to the mother ship.

DATE DUE

GAYLORD			PRINTED IN U.S.A.